PAUL

FORRESTAC

Minceur Exquise

Minceur Exquise

MICHEL GUÉRARD

WITH ALAIN COUMONT

Translated from the French by Colette Rossant

PYRAMID BOOKS

Editors: **Nicola Hill and Isobel Holland**
Art Editor: **Lisa Tai**
Production Controller: **Helen Seccombe**
Picture Researcher: **Jenny Faithful**

First published in 1992 by Pyramid Books,
an imprint of Reed International Books Limited,
Michelin House, 81 Fulham Road,
London, SW3 6RB

Published by arrangement with Pantheon Books,
A Division of Random House, Inc.

© Editions Robert Laffont, S.A., Paris, 1989

© Design Reed International Books Limited 1992

A catalogue record for this book is available from the
British Library

ISBN 1 855100 48 7

Produced by Mandarin Offset
Printed and bound in Hong Kong

Contents

*i*NTRODUCTION
DE MICHEL GUÉRARD

BY ALEXANDRE LAZAREFF

The best chefs are artists in their own right. To be successful in this field requires a lifetime of frustration, experimentation, discovery and progress. Michel Guérard's own experience has resulted in *Minceur Exquise*, this extensive collection of recipes that has already won acclaim from the culinary world.

EARLY LIFE

Michel Guérard was born 42 miles north-west of Paris in the town of Vétheuil on 27 March 1933. His father died when Michel was only two years old, and his mother remarried a butcher. Because times were hard and money short, it was difficult for her to look after two small children. Michel was sent far away to live with his grandmother. He remained with her until he was five.

It was a happy time, as Michel's grandmother was delighted to have him there. She considered him an ideal companion and spoiled him by serving a wide variety of refined dishes typical of *cuisine bourgeoise*. These included *blanquettes* and *boeuf modes* as well as Savoyard cakes and pastries whose aroma alone could make Michel's mouth water.

Soon after, the war broke out which changed everything. Michel's stepfather came to take Michel and his grandmother back to Normandy.

6

A young Michel Guérard with his brother

It was a frightening period, with night-time bombings, and the food rationing left Michel with bittersweet memories of the plentiful meals he had shared with his grandmother. By necessity he learned to economize and to get by. His family made pâtés out of the previous day's leftovers and saved the top layer of fresh milk to make *petits beurres* (shortbread). These difficult times taught Michel to fend for himself and make the most of what was available.

His stepfather left to fight in the war, and his mother ran the butcher's shop by herself. Michel helped to slaughter the animals and cut the meat, learning to distinguish the liver of a heifer from the liver of a cow. His interest in the work began to grow, and soon even the hardest jobs no longer daunted him. It was a difficult childhood, yet Michel knew that he was indispensable to the survival of his family.

At school the butcher's son was not popular with the teachers, and his marks reflected this fact. When his stepfather returned home Michel was sent as a boarder to a school in Rouen, the Lycée Corneille de Rouen, as a punishment for his poor marks, a move that was also intended to get him away from the previous negative academic atmosphere. He stayed there for two years, time enough to discover that he had a passion for the natural sciences, and he dreamed of studying to become a doctor but his stepfather tried to make him understand that the time had come for him to work. Michel's brother had already decided to become a butcher; Michel was required to choose his profession.

THE CAREER TAKES SHAPE

*F*aced with this pressure, Michel chose to return to his first love – *pâtisserie* – and became an apprentice to a *pâtissier* named Kléber Alix in Mantes-La-Jolie in Normandy.

The return to reality was brutal. His working day began at 6 A.M. on weekdays, 4 A.M. on Saturdays and 3 A.M. on Sundays, and continued late into the evening. Being young and eager, Michel was willing to do everything, even if it meant being whacked for not washing the pastry mould properly. He was often punished, though not maliciously. His pride made him accept everything dished out to him, and he came to respect and to learn from his hard-working employer.

Kléber Alix certainly had a tremendous amount to teach. He did everything himself – as well as making all the pastries, he also prepared *les plats de traiteur* (speciality dishes). He slaughtered the calves himself to make veal *quenelles*, stored eggs in lime to preserve them for the winter, and prepared the snails. He took his apprentices out with him to poach wild boars. He distilled his own alcohol illegally. And after this raw but invaluable training, Michel won first prize in the national culinary apprentice competition.

Then it was time for his military service in the French Navy, which lasted 27 months because of the Algerian war. Michel Guérard didn't actually leave France during this period; his time was divided between a vacation base for officers' children and the kitchen of the Naval Circle Club in Cherbourg. His commanding officer took a liking to him and asked him to try to transform the kitchen and run it in a cost-effective manner. Michel accepted the challenge and then proceeded to devour all the cookery books at the municipal library, especially the Larousse dictionary of cooking, which he read and reread. For this self-motivated, self-educated man, the history of France was beautifully illustrated by the history of its cuisine.

Once his military service was over, Michel became head chef at the Hotel Crillon in Paris at an exceptionally young age. There he discovered the oppressive hierarchy of a palatial kitchen and experienced the superior attitude of the regular chefs towards the *pâtisserie* chefs. He earned the respect of the sauce chef and the pantry chef by demanding that they knock before entering the *pâtisserie* room. Normally chefs remain restricted to their speciality, but Michel was quickly adopted by the older chefs and soon began to learn more – through active participation – about the various facets of *haute cuisine* from his colleagues.

Michel Guérard in his French naval uniform at the time when he was in military service

Guérard tastes a sauce

However, the arrival of an outside chef hired to reinforce the already large staff preparing a dinner for the Queen of England was the last blow to Michel's pride. He decided to enter the national competition for *le Meilleur Ouvrier de France en Pâtisserie*, and won the highly prestigious first prize.

He did not stop there, and decided to go to work at the Lido as a *pâtisserie* chef for a year. He had been fascinated by the world of the theatre ever since his tentative attempts at acting during the charity dinners of his youth, and he adored creating extravagant and dramatic cakes. At the Lido drama reigned, and Michel learned the art of putting on a spectacular culinary performance. Shortly after his arrival, he was invited to cook for the owner of the Lido, Joseph Clerico, at his parties at the Château de Villepreux. One thing led to another, and Michel stayed at the Lido for six years rather than for one as planned. He won the acclaim of Paris society. It was like being in a cocoon for Michel. Somebody was proud to have him as their chef, and enjoyed showing him off, rather like the aristocratic families of the eighteenth century.

He left the Lido for another lighthearted venture – setting up a de luxe snack bar at Antonio's, the fashionable hairstylist who sent Rolls Royces to pick up his clients. This mini-restaurant was called La Ligne (which means The Figure) and was frequented by habitués of the worlds of high fashion and refined cuisine. But all of this wasn't really serious enough. Michel was bored and wanted to go into business himself.

LE POT-AU-FEU

O n an impulse Michel bought a bankrupt bistro in Asnières, a suburb of Paris, for 20,000 francs. He named it Le Pot-au-Feu. The surroundings were dubious and a murder had recently been committed on the first floor of the building. On the day the bistro opened, 6 June 1965, the only three customers to show up were forced to jump over the legs of three African workers sleeping in the doorway.

To begin with, it was awful. Nobody was interested in refined cooking and Michel was obliged to sell coffee and sandwiches to the workers at the neighbouring rivet factory. With no money to spare, he went to nearby Genevilliers and picked flowers to brighten up the bistro. Unable to pay someone to carry his supplies back from Les Halles, he was forced to transport them himself.

The situation seemed hopeless when one day his good friend and close confidant Jean Delaveyne, the chef at Camélia in Bougival, gave him some very sound advice. 'You won't succeed this way. You are selling what everyone else sells. Make the dishes that you want to make.'

The next day Michel Guérard rewrote the menu to suit himself, and suddenly, through simple word of mouth, the restaurant became packed full of customers and journalists. The *Guide Michelin* gave it a one-star rating in 1967 and two stars in 1971. In 1968 Henri Gault made it all the rage by writing a review of its *pâté d'anguilles à la mousse de cresson* in *Paris-Presse*. The thirty-person restaurant was soon booked up a month in advance. To add a table for six, Michel had to block off the door so that customers entered through the courtyard where the toilets were located. This somewhat perilous and bizarre path into the Pot-au-Feu accentuated its Parisian ambience. Even Ted Kennedy sat and waited for two hours one night.

A cornucopia with iced fruits – an example of Guérard's creative presentation of food

The small kitchen became a veritable laboratory. Michel Guérard dared to use *foie gras* instead of oil in his vinaigrette dressing. It was at the Pot-au-Feu that he created the *salade gourmande*, frequently copied nowadays, a mixture of green beans, asparagus, truffles and *foie gras*. Michel combined duck's liver with turnips and truffles in the days when it was unthinkable to serve duck's liver with anything but apples or raisins. He invented a purée of scallops when no one ever ate anything but whole scallops. He steamed sea bass in seaweed so that it would have more of an aroma of the sea.

This creative flair extended to the presentation of the food as well. Michel introduced to his dining room individual servings on plates, as there was not enough

11

room for the *maître d'* to cut and serve the meat in the dining room itself. He was very interested in the aestheticism of his dishes, the edible colours as beautiful as a painting, and he strove to create a unique culinary masterpiece with each dish.

Guérard (top centre) and friends in the courtyard outside the Pot-au Feu

NOUVELLE CUISINE

Paul Bocuse and the Troisgros brothers adopted Michel after a meal at the Pot-au-Feu, and he saw them often. But most of all it was Michel's friend Jean Delaveyne who joined him in blazing around the kitchen and inventing new dishes. It was a time of conspiracy and cooperation, when Parisian chefs would plot together in each other's kitchens after a full night's work. Jacques Manière and Alain Senderens soon joined the new culinary movement. This melting pot of talent resembled the *Bâteau Lavoir* period for the Cubist painters. The food critics Henri Gault and Christian Millau invented a name for the movement, *la nouvelle cuisine.*

This concept was a journalistic creation. *Nouvelle cuisine* was above all a flash point, a sign of revolt, a reaction rather than a concerted action. Certain chefs such as Paul Bocuse and, to a lesser degree, the Troisgros brothers, remained more traditional in their approach. But they all had a desire to be innovative, to move away from those who unquestioningly followed the teachings of Escoffier.

Escoffier had wanted to codify French cuisine. The *Maîtres Cuisiniers* (an organization of French chefs) followed his instructions to the letter and believed that his principles should be upheld. They considered that the new school violated tradition, and was an insult to Escoffier's memory. It seemed impossible to introduce anything new to French cuisine, as the *Maîtres Cuisiniers* would inevitably condemn it.

The young chefs, who didn't share this enthusiasm for preserving tradition, longed to break away. But the mere desire for freedom did not amount to an agenda. They began by switching to individual servings (on plates instead of platters), which permitted them to arrange the food aesthetically. They also found that sauces could be lightened by reducing the quantities

Michel Guérard being supported by legendary chef Paul Bocuse

of butter, cream and eggs used, that cooking time could be shortened, fish barely cooked and vegetables served *al dente*. With the arrival of Teflon pans, they were able to cook without fats. They began to rely more on *mousses* (purées) and *coulis* (strained sauces).

However, the movement still lacked unity. It would be some time before Michel Guérard could take his creation a step further, let this fledgling doctrine mature, and establish his own specific branch of *nouvelle cuisine, cuisine minceur*. For this fate had to take a hand and put the entire enterprise in question.

Due to the construction of a local road, Michel was forced out of the Pot-au-Feu. He negotiated firmly on the subject of his land and obtained more money for his restaurant than he would have had he sold it. He then began to look in Paris for a prestigious address that would allow him to keep his faithful clientele.

THE REGINSKAÏA

*I*n the meantime, the nightclub singer Régine asked him to start a Russian cabaret in Paris called the Reginskaïa. It was certainly a challenge, as *haute cuisine* chefs do not normally go to work in a cabaret. In addition, an entire kitchen needed to be installed and a full staff assembled. The results were mixed, due to lack of preparation. The opening was held prematurely and the critics accused Michel Guérard of inconsistency. It was not a complete waste of time, however, as he succeeded in earning the friendship of Régine, who would later launch clubs in both Paris and New York and, more significantly, he also met his future wife, Christine Barthélémy, during a dinner at the cabaret.

GUÉRARD MEETS HIS FUTURE WIFE

*H*e was 39 years old, she was 28 and had graduated from *Hautes Etudes Commerciales*, the best business school in France. It was love at first sight. Michel still marvels today at this opportune pairing of a chef and an intellectual. It was perfect timing, as Christine was running Eugénie-les-Bains, a spa resort she had just acquired from her father, Adrien Barthélémy. A remarkable self-made man, Barthélémy had recently invented the Biotherm range and created the first chain of French spa resorts, a chain which now successfully holds 20 per cent of the market.

Michel went to look at Eugénie-les-Bains with Christine. and was struck by the clinical atmosphere of the resort, as well as by the overweight clients who were trying desperately to slim down by eating grated carrots! He wondered what dishes he would be able to prepare for them. The thought lingered, as he decided that inventing an entirely new diet would be an excellent way to impress, and thus seduce, his future wife. Not knowing anything about the dietary world, he ploughed through nutritional, diet and medical books. Patiently, discreetly, he began to experiment with new recipes. He did not, however, have the slightest intention of going to work at Eugénie-les-Bains.

The sign as you approach Eugénie-les-Bains proclaiming it to be the first minceur village of France

He continued to comb Paris for a suitably prestigious address. At one point he was tempted to buy Laperouse. Then, more seriously, he joined forces with Gaston Lenôtre in a bid for Laurent, that magical pavilion on the Champs Elysées, but James Goldsmith outbid them. As for his attempt to buy Maxim's, Michel was overtaken by Pierre Cardin. Having gone from failure to failure, he asked himself, why not move out and cook at Eugénie-les-Bains? Christine was delighted.

EUGÉNIE-LES-BAINS AND CUISINE MINCEUR

The challenge posed by Eugénie-les-Bains was not unlike Michel's wartime experience of austerity. How, with so many dietary restrictions, could he possibly come up with delicious dishes? How could he function creatively within such calorie-conscious limitations? He wanted to design a healthy diet that wouldn't give people the feeling of being in hospital: he wanted to serve food that was a pleasure both to look at and to eat. This new style of cooking needed to be similar to *nouvelle cuisine* but even better. Thus *cuisine minceur* was born.

The insurmountable problem seemed to be sauces, the cornerstones of French cooking. Rich sauces provide both taste and variety, but a lighter, different type of sauce had to be discovered. Eliminating both cream and butter would be difficult but a less fatty substitute had to be found. Yogurt was too acidic, and *fromage blanc* too dry. No formula seemed to satisfy Michel. Yet purées made from vegetables such as carrots, mushrooms and leeks had the desired consistency, and were an aesthetic plus too, as each vegetable represented an additional colour on his culinary palette.

Eventually, substitutes were found for all forbidden products. In the *mousse au fenouil* (fennel purée), egg whites replaced whipped cream. The *hachis parmentier* (mixed meat with potato purée), which was normally so rich with truffles and veal sweetbreads, could be made without mashed potatoes by substituting a celeriac and cauliflower purée. Even mayonnaise could be made lighter by adding *fromage blanc*.

In terms of cooking time, the lessons learned at the Pot-au-Feu came in

The menu at Eugénie-les-Bains

The hotel Les Prés et les Sources d'Eugénie

handy. Existing fats in food needed to be eliminated if possible. The use of Teflon pans became *de rigueur*. Chicken skins were pierced in order to lose fat and add flavour. Steamers were used to enhance the aroma of fish, with seaweed added to sea bass and pine nuts and wild mint to trout.

In general, fish and seafood are the staples of a low-calorie diet. But Michel refused to exclude either grilled meats or poultry in his quest. Attention to detail was applied to all products used in Michel Guérard's kitchen. A herb garden was planted to ensure the freshness and quality of all the herbs, one local woman grew some of the vegetables, and another supplied the flowers and the tomatoes. All the gardeners used natural fertilizers according to precise instructions. The bread was made in the village by a local baker under strict surveillance. Michel's apprenticeships had left their mark.

Grilling lobsters on the open hearth in the restaurant kitchen

Even bread, at that time considered anything but slimming, was not excluded from the menu, as Michel understood that fibre is an essential part of a healthy diet. The problem of dessert, however, proved more complex.

Replacing sugar was simple, as artificial sweeteners, especially aspartame, have proved a blessing. Butter was replaced too by some new products that add the flavour without the fat. Light purées and mousses were also freely incorporated into the diet. But Michel Guérard still wasn't completely satisfied. The *pâtisserie* chef could not rest until he had achieved the ultimate aim – to make traditional French desserts without excess.

So he schemed. A *Paris-Brest*, for example, is a choux pastry ring with pralined butter and grilled almonds. For the low-calorie version, Michel Guérard kept the choux ring and filled it with egg whites, artificial sweetener, and a dash of whipped cream. It was then flavoured with coffee, although naturally the grilled almonds had to be omitted. One day he concocted a rum baba in the same spirit by using a base syrup made from sugar substitute, and flavouring it with verbena.

This *cuisine minceur* seemed both a revelation and a revolution. When it was officially launched in 1974 Michel Guérard was unanimously hailed by the critics. On 9 February 1976 he received the accolade of appearing on the cover of *Time* magazine. Eleven years later in February 1987 the *Sunday Times* magazine labelled him one of the 20 personalities that had shaped the previous 15 years. He was the only French person to be included. Soon afterwards he was awarded a third Michelin star. He put his theory and his diet down in writing with *La Grande Cuisine Minceur* (published in the UK as *Cuisine Minceur*), followed by *La Cuisine Gourmande* (published in the UK as *Michel Guérard's Cuisine Gourmande*). Both books were highly successful and were translated into twelve languages. For the first time a chef had made his remarkable

On 9 February 1976 Guérard found himself on the cover of Time *magazine, an accolade which none of his contemporaries or indeed any other chef has so far managed to achieve*

recipes accessible to amateur cooks by writing them down in easily understood language and using everyday products. Here we can see the influence of Christine Guérard.

After a preliminary television appearance on a programme called *La Grande Cocotte* with Claude Jolly-Lebey, Jean Ferniot and chefs Bocuse, Troisgros and Vergé, Michel Guérard earned a regular slot on Anne-Marie Peysson's popular show, which was broadcast weekly on Saturday lunchtimes. Michel Guérard later published these recipes in 1982 as *Mes Recettes à la Télé* (published in France by Robert Laffont). He was a founding member of the Chambre Syndicale de la Haute Cuisine Française, and later became the first president of the Conseil National des Arts Culinaires. He was finally awarded the legion of honour in 1990.

However, this man, with all his honours and responsibilities, wanted most of all just to be a chef. Guérard continued to experiment with new recipes, and to create new dishes, and he flatly refused to become a slave to the *cuisine minceur* doctrine that he himself had created.

Everything interested him. A trip to China in 1978 with Jean Claude Lebey, Alain Senderens, Alain Chapel and Pierre Troisgros opened up a whole new world. Discovering how to prepare lacquered duck was a revelation. On his return, he made truffle ravioli fashionable at the same time as Senderens independently created his own ravioli. He discovered Chinese woks and added new ingredients to his culinary repertoire such as ginger, Chinese mushrooms, soy sauce and oyster sauce, but always in subtle amounts so that they served merely to enhance the flavours of traditional French cuisine.

CUISINE GOURMANDE

Outside the dietary field he liked to work on what he called *cuisine gourmande*. This 'food-lover's cuisine', however, was not a systematic diet like *cuisine minceur* but rather the natural expression of Guérard's love for his craft. To paraphrase Claude Monet, he likes to say that he 'cooks like the bird sings'. This carefree, happy and irreverent diet was the natural evolution of a concept that started back in the days of Jean Delaveyne with a distaste for the limitations of classic cuisine. One of Michel Guérard's striking characteristics is that he is constantly creating. Even while eating lunch he will be observing the colour and texture of the food. He has fun with his creations. 'I like asparagus, I like truffles and asparagus. I like iodine. I decided to create a new cold dish: cod in fish soup with oysters, asparagus and a vinaigrette made with truffles. A tailored poached egg will be the final touch. I create a recipe the way other people compose songs.'

This romanticism and passion developed into a business venture – des Prés d'Eugénie, an enterprise created by Christine and Michel Guérard. More than 80 million francs were invested in transforming this old-fashioned building into a Louisiana-style Relais Château equipped with a complex modern thermal bath system. The original staff of 20 grew to 130. Christine and Michel Guérard now run 12 other spa resorts, though Eugénie-les-Bains remains the jewel in the crown.

WORKING WITH NESTLÉ

In 1976 the head of Nestlé asked Michel Guérard to create a new range of frozen foods for Findus. At first he was hesitant, but a visit to the factory in Beauvais quickly convinced him of the high standards of both production and staff. So, as he had in his involvement with Régine, he

The sumptuous decor is inspired by Christine Guérard and is a subtle blend of antique and modern. The portrait here is of the Empress Eugénie

put his professional reputation at risk and accepted the challenge. He does not regret having been the first chef to explore the possibilities of the frozen food industry.

Once he became involved, a new and unfamiliar world opened up to him – one based on precision, marketing, and a rigorous commercialism that was far removed from the empiricism of the chefs with whom he was accustomed to working. He learned that in order to create a dish successfully he had to take into account the needs of the commercial sector and the marketing team, as well as industrial and bacteriological constraints, available supplies, and manufacturing cost. Accustomed to independent creation, Michel Guérard now had to adapt to testing regulations – in consultation with the heads of Findus, the sales team, the research and development team, and the focus group taste-testers.

He learned that freezing food can modify the characteristics of the ingredients. It can sometimes cause dehydration, a dulling of flavour, a change in the molecular structure or oxydation, bacteriological differences and even colour changes. A product that is normally creamy-white can turn an unappetizing brown when frozen. Once again Michel Guérard flourished creatively under constraints. He came up with bestselling dishes such as *pithiviers de poissons* (a type of fish cake) and *sauce au beurre blanc et au citron* (a white butter and lemon sauce). His products generated ten per cent of Findus' sales.

His collaboration with Nestlé went beyond Findus. He was involved in developing a range of low-calorie dishes called Lean Cuisine (a joint venture with the American subsidiary), worked on Maggi dehydrated products, and improved the quality of Gervais ice-cream. He created elaborate ready-made dishes for the British subsidiary Chambourcy but unfortunately these proved too expensive for the market. He found the time to travel to the United States and sell his own brand of chocolates there for three years and, with his customary persistence, he organized tastings and displays in supermarkets in 30 American cities. He also tried to launch *comptoirs gourmands* (gourmet food shops) in Paris and Lyons with the textile company DMC.

Michel Guérard's name adorns the wall outside Les Prés et les Sources d'Eugénie

*Michel Guérard's latest passion –
winemaking – here he can be seen with
some of his grape harvest*

CUISINE DE SANTÉ

This extensive involvement with the industrial world forced Michel Guérard to reconsider his own style of cooking. Working alongside researchers he brought with him, he tried to develop a *cuisine de santé* (health-conscious cuisine) – a combination of *cuisine gourmande, cuisine minceur* and convenience foods. The idea behind developing a healthy diet was that people could lose a few pounds without obsessive calorie counting. Furthermore, Michel Guérard dreamed of putting together a balanced diet that would delay loss of eyesight, help to prevent cancer and cardiovascular problems, and help people lose weight in specific areas of the body. Certain ingredients and food combinations might be more effective in slimming down heavy thighs than the buttocks, or work more quickly on the hips than the stomach, and so on.

While exploring these avenues, fascinating in themselves, Michel Guérard embarked on a new challenge – making his own wine.

BECOMING A WINE PRODUCER

He discovered wine-making late in life while living in the beautiful seventeenth-century Bachen residence he had recently acquired. At the age of 50 he returned to school two days a week for seven months at the Institut d'Oenologie de la Faculté des Sciences in Bordeaux. Enthusiastically he studied the geographical analysis of soil and learned more about vines, clones, stock and climatic statistics. He also learned how to define the personality of a wine, and decided on the taste components he would like to produce in his own wine. He brought home folders crammed full of notes and ideas about wine as well as new recipe ideas, such as *les piccatas de morue douce grillée*, inspired by his knowledge of wine.

This student prodigy refused to accept *la régle du cépage unique* (the law of singular vine usage) imposed in the Tursan vineyard. Instead he made his wine the way one usually makes Bordelais, by mixing several vines. He was lucky enough to meet Jean Claude Berroue – the oenologist of the Château Pétrus – who helped him create a new Tursan wine in the old-fashioned manner by using the four trademark vines. He prepared his wine in the same way as he prepared his dishes by adding, dividing, transforming. Thus was born Michel Guérard's first white wine, the *Baron de Bachen*, soon to be followed by a second, *Le Château de Baron*. To do justice to these wines, Michel Guérard commissioned from two young architects, Jean de Gastines and Patrick Dillon (who have since become experts on wine architecture), a magnificent classical Greek structure supported and surrounded by ornate columns opening on to a magnificent amphitheatre in which he could house his wines.

A theatre for wine – this was the ultimate dream of Michel Guérard, the only chef to have cooked in a major hotel, a cabaret and a top-class restaurant, as well as in the food production industry, and the only one to have explored thoroughly both slimming and sumptuously rich cuisine.

Like the painters with whom he identifies, Michel Guérard has passed through several 'periods', several stages of creation. Each one of these periods has been marked by the publication of a book.

A bottle of Baron de Bachen, Guérard's first white wine

The magnificent classic Greek structure supported and surrounded by ornate columns opening on to a splendid amphitheatre in which Guérard houses his wines

This book marks not only the development of Michel Guérard's own talent but also the evolution of the popular principles of healthy eating. Since the success of his book *Cuisine Minceur*, the concept of a well-balanced, fitness-oriented diet is no longer contested but has become standard practice. Ten years of creative cuisine at Eugénie-les-Bains have encouraged Michel Guérard to record his discoveries. While all the dishes offered in this book are of course low calorie, it is important to remember that the final objective is more to do with eating a balanced diet than just losing weight.

Minceur Exquise was written in collaboration with Alain Coumont, a student of Michel Guérard who worked for two years at Eugénie-les-Bains and was converted to the *cuisine minceur* cause. With her special skill for adapting chef's recipes for everyday use, Martine Jolly has helped to make the recipes more accessible. Together these talents have perfected and simplified the step-by-step preparation of the following recipes.

COOKING METHODS

When he discovered fire, man soon realized that he could use it, not only for warmth and protection, but also as a brilliant means of transforming an inspired raw ingredient into a tasty dish. No doubt he started off by grilling and searing before finding out about slower cooking methods such as burying food in the ashes of his fire and by boiling it in water in rudimentary pots. Eventually he hit upon the idea of making an oven out of clay or stones buried in the ground to cook his venison by a diffused heat.

These are the same cooking methods that, slowly refined over the years, we practise today. Now we have all the equipment necessary for cooking with water or steam and for sautéeing, frying or stewing, roasting and grilling.

Most ingredients lend themselves to different cooking methods. All one needs to know is how to cook them well and to respect the basic principles of each method. In this book we shall be looking at methods of cooking suitable for *cuisine minceur*.

GRILLING

Good heat conduction is the basis of perfect grilling. It is a very suitable method for *cuisine minceur* provided that the article to be grilled is very lightly oiled first and patted with kitchen paper after cooking to absorb excess fat.

When cooking poultry, prick the skin to allow the fat to run out.

To minimize fat, do not oil meat at all, but soak it in water flavoured with thyme, sage or other herbs before grilling.

GRILLING FISH

PREPARATION: with a brush, lightly oil all sides of the fish. Ensure that the grill pan is perfectly clean and oil this too.
TEMPERATURE: very hot for small fish such as sardines, herrings, soles, dabs and mackerel; slightly cooler for large fish, such as sea bream, salmon and turbot.
TIPS:
• For *cuisine minceur*, grilling is the best method of cooking oily and semi-oily fish, such as sardines, mackerel and herrings, as it helps them to lose some of their oiliness.
• When cooking flat fish, place the white skin side on the grill first. For round fish, place on the grill with the spine to the left first.

• Large fish, such as salmon and cod, can be cut into steaks and grilled on both sides at a high temperature.
• A salmon may be grilled whole by cutting it lengthwise along the back into strips 5-6 cm/2-2½ inches wide, taking care to keep the skin on. Slash and lightly oil the skin and place skin side down under a hot grill. It will cook through and remain tender left in this position.

GRILLING RED MEATS

PREPARATION: the grill pan must be clean.
Make sure the meat is at room temperature; if it comes straight from the refrigerator it will still be cold in the centre after grilling which would not be good. Lightly brush the meat and the grill pan with oil.
TEMPERATURE: very hot.
There are four levels of cooking red meat:
• **Blue:** by fast cooking. Put the meat on the grill rack, then give it a half turn to seal it and form a squared pattern on the outside. Turn it over and repeat with the other side. When touched, the meat is soft. To warm it right through, take it away from the direct heat and keep covered for a few moments in a warm place.
• **Rare:** keep the meat under the grill a little longer. Turn it over when you see drops of blood coming to the surface. The meat is less soft to touch.
• **Medium:** grill at a slightly lower heat which will penetrate right through the meat, bringing more drops of blood to the surface. The meat is firmer to the touch.
• **Well done:** the meat is cooked longer under a moderate heat and the blood will ooze out all over the surface. When cooked it is very firm to the touch.

GRILLING WHITE MEATS AND POULTRY

PREPARATION: again, the grill pan must be scrupulously clean and lightly oiled with a brush.
TEMPERATURE: a very hot pre-heated grill, but using a less fierce heat than for red meat.
Care must be taken with white meats and poultry to avoid drying out and toughness. To achieve this, such meat is cooked more slowly to the point where it is pale pink in the middle. At this point, a needle inserted into it will produce drops of almost colourless juice. Remove from the grill and

leave covered in a warm place for a few moments.

TIPS:

• Do not salt meat before cooking, but only after it has browned. Salt added too soon draws out the blood and prevents browning.

• With large joints of meat, cut into pieces, then season.

• Use a spatula to turn the meat, not a fork, to prevent blood running out.

• Large pieces must be grilled more slowly to cook right through. Grill under a lower heat.

• In principle, grilled meat should be served with the side that was cooked first uppermost.

POACHING

This is a simple method of cooking by plunging ingredients into liquid which can be plain water, a meat or fish stock, or a syrup.

Poaching is often used in *cuisine minceur* as all fat is eliminated, but that does not mean that the taste is eliminated too. A lobster, cooked in water sufficiently salted to resemble the sea, keeps all its fine flavour. Stocks, that have been well skimmed to minimize fat, give their flavour to the food being poached and can often then be used to make light sauces or tasty soups.

Poaching may be started in either cold or hot liquid.

COLD WATER

The food is not seared by the heat, so it imparts its flavour into the water and enriches it. This is the principle behind stews and stocks made with poultry, fish and shellfish.

HOT WATER

Exactly the opposite principle is employed here: by searing the food in a hot liquid all its flavour and goodness is retained. Thus, green vegetables are cooked in plenty of boiling salted water, and fruits in hot syrup.

STEAMING

This is a method of cooking whereby the food is cooked in the steam emitted from boiling water in a closed pan.

Salted water is used most often, but an aromatic stock is also effective and can afterwards be used as the basis of an accompanying sauce.

This method offers real advantages to *cuisine minceur*. Steaming in an enclosed pan allows the food to retain all its flavour and goodness without the addition of fat.

METHOD:

• Use a steamer with several compartments.

• If a conventional steamer is unavailable, a folding-basket type steamer can be held in place in the pan.

• Fill the pan with the cooking liquid until it just reaches the base of the steaming compartment, and bring to the boil.

• Put the food into the steaming compartment, close the lid tightly to allow the steam to penetrate the food.

Following the same method, the steaming basket may be covered with seaweed or herbs when cooking fish, or hay for lamb or ham. Place the meat or fish on top and cover with more of the same flavourings. Sprinkle with water to aid the steaming process, then cover tightly. The food will cook gently, bathed in aromatic steam.

COOKING IN PARCELS (EN PAPILLOTE)

The food to be cooked is laid on very lightly oiled foil or greaseproof paper, with a few added ingredients, such as a little stock, herbs or seasonings, according to the recipe. The foil or paper is then folded up into a crescent shape with the edges well pinched together to form a hermetic seal.

For *cuisine minceur*, this method allows food to be cooked with plenty of aroma and flavour but without added fat.

The parcels may be steamed by simply putting them into a steaming basket, or they may be baked in a very hot oven on an oiled baking sheet.

BRAISING

Like steaming and the parcel method, braising is another means of cooking in an enclosed container. The food is first sealed at a high temperature, then cooked slowly and gently in a covered casserole.

Brown the meat first in a little fat, then put it into a casserole with finely chopped vegetables. Pour in an aromatic liquid until it comes half-way up the food in the pot. The meat slowly tenderizes and imparts its flavour to the juices which can then be made into an accompanying sauce.

At first sight, braising seems to be at odds with the

principles of *cuisine minceur*. This is not so, providing certain precautions are taken:
• all fat must be removed from the meat;
• after sealing, the meat is removed from the casserole and wiped with kitchen paper;
• all fat is poured off from the casserole before the meat is returned to it with the vegetables and cooking liquid.

Aim to braise the food 24 hours before it is required. Leave it overnight in the refrigerator and use a spoon to skim off the fat which has come to the surface, before reheating it slowly and thoroughly. Removing the fat will not diminish the flavour of the sauce, nor of the meat which will be very tender.

ROASTING

This is a method of cooking meat by dry heat and turning it frequently. All sides of the meat must be lightly oiled, as in grilling, to seal and brown.

This method can be achieved in an oven or on a spit.

Like grilling, this method is perfectly satisfactory for *cuisine minceur*, provided the usual precautions are observed.
• Do not let the butcher wrap the joint in strips of fat. It will be cooked at a high temperature.
• Oil the joint very lightly, using just enough to prevent it burning as it browns.
• For poultry, prick the skin to allow the fat to run out.
• Before making gravy or sauce pour off all the fat from the pan. Cover the joint and let it rest for 15-20 minutes. The juices which then run out can be used as the basis for the sauce.

IN THE OVEN

Preheat the oven to the temperature required, according to the type of meat and its weight. Lightly oil the joint, but do not season it. Place it either directly in a roasting dish, or on a bed of ground bones (or seaweed if cooking fish), or on a rack over a roasting dish to prevent the joint from standing in its own fat. After the meat has browned, reduce the temperature and baste with the juices. Salt may be added at this point. The temperature should be lowered still further for white meats and poultry to prevent toughness.

SPIT-ROASTING

This is cooking over a fire, with the food surrounded by dry air. Proceed in the same way as for oven-roasting, taking care to baste the food frequently to avoid drying out.

TIPS:
• The joint will be more tender and have a more uniform colour if it is left to rest, covered in a foil 'tent' after cooking.
• For a good gravy, remove the joint, cover and keep warm. Pour off most of the fat from the dripping tray below the spit (the gravy will blend more easily if about a quarter of the fat is left). 'Deglaze' the pan – that is, add to it twice the volume of water than the required amount of gravy and stir, scraping up all the meat residues as you do so. Bring to the boil and reduce by half (allow 2 tablespoons per person). Pass through a fine sieve and add a few drops of good red wine vinegar to finish.

STOCKS

These are flavoured liquids obtained by slowly boiling (simmering) meat, vegetables and aromatic ingredients which have been allowed to soak in cold water.

Light stocks (*bouillons*) are an essential ingredient of many dishes, stews and casseroles in particular.

Equally in classic cooking and in *cuisine minceur*, a really good stock is obtained by passing it through a fine sieve to get rid of any scraps, and then refrigerated to allow the fat to come to the surface, which can then easily be skimmed off with a spoon.

These are excellent liquids for stewing and can also be used for steaming. Stocks keep for 2-3 days in the refrigerator, several months in a freezer.

Stocks (*fonds*) are prepared in the same way as light stocks, but allowed to simmer longer to develop a stronger flavour. With this type of stock, only the final liquid is used for cooking purposes, so meat intended for the table is not included; rather, use ground bones, meat trimmings, poultry carcasses and giblets to which vegetables and aromatic seasonings are added.

Again, the stock should be passed through a fine sieve, then refrigerated and the fat skimmed off before use.

These techniques do demand a little time and effort, but it is well worth devoting an afternoon to preparing stock for the beneficial effect it will have on your cooking. Afterwards, nothing could be simpler than to freeze little pots of stock to be used at a later date as an indispensable ingredient in sauces and casseroles.

There is a difference between *fonds blonds* (golden stock) and *fonds blancs* (pale stock). The former are obtained by browning bones, meat trimmings and giblets in the oven before putting them into the water, to give the stock a golden colour. For the latter, the bones and trimmings go straight into the pot with the vegetables, wine and water.

GOLDEN VEAL STOCK

To make 1 litre/1¾ pints of stock:

1 kg/2¼ lb ground veal bones
500 g/1¼ lb beef trimmings
50 g/2 oz raw ham
100 g/4 oz carrots, cut into small cubes
100 g/4 oz mushrooms, cut into small cubes
50 g/2 oz onions, cut into small cubes
15 g/½ oz celery, cut into small cubes
1 shallot, finely chopped
1 clove of garlic, crushed
125 ml/4 fl oz dry white wine
2 litres/3½ pints cold water
2 tomatoes, seeded
1 tablespoon tomato purée
1 bouquet garni
1 teaspoon chervil
½ teaspoon tarragon

Preparation time: 20 minutes
Cooking time: first process – 25-30 minutes;
second process – 3-4 hours

FIRST PROCESS: brown the bones on a baking sheet for 15 minutes in a very hot oven, without any fat. Turn several times during cooking, using a small metal spoon. Add the beef trimmings, ham, carrots, mushrooms, onions, celery, shallot and garlic. Put back in the oven to 'sweat' (ie to heat without colouring) for 5 minutes.

SECOND PROCESS: put the bones and vegetables in a saucepan or small casserole. Add the wine and boil until it has almost completely evaporated.

Add the cold water, tomatoes, tomato purée, bouquet garni and herbs.

Simmer slowly for 3-4 hours, skimming the surface frequently to draw off the fat and impurities.

Pass the liquid (there should be about 1 litre/1¾ pints) through a fine sieve into a bowl.

To ensure the elimination of all fat, put the bowl into the refrigerator. The fat will rise to the surface and can easily be skimmed off.

USES: as a base for numerous sauces, as a liquid (or an addition to the cooking liquid) for dishes such as stews, *coq au vin*, fish stews and *fricassées*.

TIP: to make this stock thicker, it can be blended by using the following method:
• In a small cup, mix a tablespoon of arrowroot with 50 ml/ 2 fl oz of water or white wine.
• Slowly pour this mixture into the boiling stock, whisking to avoid lumps.
• Gently bring the stock to the boil and reduce to half the quantity by evaporation. During this time, any remaining impurities will rise to the surface and must be skimmed off with a ladle or skimming spoon.
• This golden veal stock can then be used as a base for sauces where alcohol is added, then almost completely evaporated, or added to a roasting tin in which meat or poultry has been roasted, to be blended with the delicious meat residues.

MEAT GLAZE

Another way of producing a thick stock, without blending, is to simmer slowly 1 litre/1¾ pints of veal stock over a low heat, skimming the top all the time, until it has reduced to a tenth of its initial volume. The glaze is perfect when it leaves a glistening coating on the back of a spoon. It is ideal for livening up any rather uninteresting dish.

GOLDEN POULTRY STOCK

Prepare in the same way as golden veal stock, replacing the veal bones with a duck's carcass, browned in the oven.

PALE POULTRY STOCK

To make 1 litre/1¾ pints of stock:

1 kg/2¼ lb broken carcasses of chicken or other poultry
100 g/4 oz mushrooms, finely chopped
100 g/4 oz carrots, finely chopped
1 shallot, finely chopped
l leek
1 small stick of celery
1 clove of garlic, crushed
100 ml/3½ fl oz dry white wine
2 litres/3½ pints cold water
1 bouquet garni
1 small white onion
1 clove

Preparation time: 15-20 minutes
Cooking time: 3 hours

Put the ground bones into a saucepan with the vegetables. Heat, add the white wine and boil until it has almost completely evaporated.

Add the cold water, bouquet garni and onion stuck with the clove. Simmer slowly over a low heat, skimming the surface frequently. Pass the stock through a fine sieve and leave in the refrigerator until needed.

PALE VEAL STOCK

This is prepared as above, replacing the chicken carcasses with the same weight of blanched veal bones (plunge into boiling water for 1 minute).

USES: in dishes requiring a white sauce such as *blanquettes*, *fricassées* and chicken in white sauce, some soups and vegetable dishes such as rice and lettuce.

GAME STOCK AND GLAZE

These are prepared in the same way as the pale veal stock and veal glaze. Use bones and trimmings from game, adding to the other ingredients 5 sprigs of juniper berries and a sprig of sage.

A jovial Guérard holds on to a cockerel

FISH *FUMET*

To make 1 litre/1¾ pints of stock:

*1 kg/2¼ lb fish bones and heads (sole for the best flavour, or
turbot, brill or whiting; avoid oily fish)
1 shallot, finely chopped
100 g/4 oz onions, thinly sliced
50 g/2 oz mushrooms, thinly sliced
25 g/1 oz butter
2 tablespoons groundnut oil
100 ml/3½ fl oz dry white wine
1.5 litres/2¾ pints cold water
salt
1 bouquet garni with plenty of parsley*

*Preparation time: 15 minutes
Cooking time: 30-35 minutes*

Unless they are very fresh, put the fish heads and bones to
soak in cold water for about 30 minutes. If using fish heads,
remove the gills before use. 'Sweat' the vegetables and lightly
ground bones in the oil and butter for 5 minutes.

Moisten with the wine and boil until it has almost
completely evaporated.

Pour on the cold water, add salt and the bouquet garni.

Bring back to the boil and simmer, uncovered, over a low
heat for 20 minutes. During this time, skim every time the
impurities form a scum on the surface.

Pass the stock (there should be 1 litre/1¾ pints) through a
fine sieve, pressing down on the bones with a small ladle.
Refrigerate until required.

FISH GLAZE: To obtain a fish glaze, follow the same method as
for a meat glaze:
• boil the stock over a low heat
• skim all the time it is being reduced
• stop cooking when about 100 ml/3½ fl oz of syrupy,
glistening liquid remains.

Store in the refrigerator.

USES: fish glaze has the same uses as meat glaze.

HOW TO ACHIEVE RAPID SUCCESS WITH THE GREAT TRADITIONAL STOCKS

Classic chicken stock can be replaced simply by a stock cube
or powder. It can then be used as a base for fish or veal
stock. The two latter stocks can then be quickly finished by
the addition of a calf's foot, and then by blending to produce
a semi-glazed stock.

SIMPLE FISH STOCK

For 500 ml/17 fl oz of fish stock:

*1 tablespoon olive oil
1 large carrot
1 large onion, cut into small cubes
100 g/4 oz button mushrooms, cut into
small cubes
crushed bones of 6 sole
1 calf's foot, cut into 8 pieces
1 bouquet garni with plenty of parsley
5 peppercorns
1 clove
2 litres/3½ pints cold water
3 chicken stock cubes*

*Preparation time: 15 minutes
Cooking time: 2 hours 10 minutes*

Put the olive oil in a warm saucepan. Add the carrot, onion
and mushrooms.

Add the fish bones, calf's foot, bouquet garni,
peppercorns and clove.

Pour on the cold water and crumble in the stock cubes.
Boil, uncovered, over a low heat for 2 hours.

Skim the surface of the stock 5 or 6 times during the
cooking period.

Pass the remaining fish stock (there should be 500 ml/18 fl
oz) through a fine sieve. The stock will be very highly
flavoured, allowing the addition of a further 250 ml/8 fl oz
water before use, if desired.

SIMPLE VEAL STOCK

For 500 ml/17 fl oz of veal stock:

1 large carrot, cut into small cubes
1 large onion, cut into small cubes
100 g/4 oz mushrooms, cut into small cubes
1 tablespoon olive oil
1 calf's foot, cut into 8 pieces
1 bouquet garni
1 clove
1 tomato, halved
15 g/½ oz dried mushrooms (for example, morels
or ceps)
1 teaspoon tomato purée
1 teaspoon arôme Patrelle (see note below)
2 litres/3½ pints water
3 chicken stock cubes
1 teaspoon cornflour
1 teaspoon water

Preparation time: 15 minutes
Cooking time: 2 hours 40 minutes

Put the carrot, onion and mushrooms in the olive oil in a warm saucepan to colour.

Add the calf's foot, bouquet garni, clove, tomato, dried mushrooms, tomato purée and arôme Patrelle (if using).

Pour in the water and crumble in the stock cubes. Boil, uncovered, over a low heat for 2½ hours. Skim off the impurities which rise to the surface 5 or 6 times during the cooking period.

At the end of the stated time, pass the remaining stock (there should be 500 ml/17 fl oz) through a fine sieve into a clean saucepan. Bring back to the boil and whisk in the cornflour mixed with the water. The veal stock is now finished and is practically a demi-glaze – and excellent it is, too. Leave overnight in the refrigerator and skim off any fat the next day.

Note: arôme Patrelle is a type of gravy browning, not often found outside France. Since it is included mainly to colour the stock, it can be omitted here.

LIAISONS

A liaison is essentially a process to transform a clear stock into a thick sauce.

In classic cuisine, rich ingredients such as a *roux* made with butter and flour, egg yolks and cream, butter, *crème fraîche*, even *foie gras* are used as thickeners. Here, we shall look only at those ingredients which are compatible with *cuisine minceur*.

STARCH: POTATO FLOUR AND CORNFLOUR: mix the starch with a little water. Quickly and steadily, add this to the boiling sauce to be thickened. You will need between 25-75 g/1-3 oz starch to 1 litre/1¾ pints of liquid. Let the sauce boil for 10-15 minutes.

EGG LIAISON: beat the egg yolks in a bowl, mix in a little of the sauce to be thickened. Pour this mixture into the sauce in the pan. Whisk and heat through slowly, taking care to ensure the mixture does not reach boiling point, which would make the eggs separate and curdle the sauce.

USES: soups, smooth soups (*veloutés*), *sauce poulette* and white sauce. More suitable for *cuisine minceur* is sabayon sauce:
• Whisk together egg yolks and water at a ratio of 4 yolks to 6 tablespoons of water.

The mixture will increase considerably in volume when the air is whisked in.

Very quickly whisk the mixture into the boiling sauce or soup that is to be thickened: the egg suspension will coagulate when it comes in contact with the hot sauce and will increase the volume whilst making it appear very light.

LIAISONS USING BLOOD, OR CORAL: blood from a pig, game or fish (lamprey); the coral from shellfish (lobster).

Follow the same technique as before, but replace the egg yolks with the blood, or the coral of a lobster (sometimes mixed first with *crème fraîche* or butter). Do not allow the liaison to boil.

USES: *coq au vin*, game or fish stews and lobster *à l'Américaine*.

LIAISONS WITH PURÉED VEGETABLES: this is a valuable method for *cuisine minceur*.

A small amount of finely puréed cooked vegetables is added to the liquid to be thickened.

These can be vegetables cooked, according to the recipe, to be served with the meat or fish, as well as a liaison for the sauce. These puréed liaisons are rich in vitamins and they are easily assimilated due to the breaking down of the cellulose during cooking, which prevents acidity. This subtle, well-proportioned mixture of vegetables is a very original way of introducing aromatic harmony to a dish.

Try creating other harmonious mixtures with a judicious blending of fruits and vegetables.

LIAISONS WITH YOGURT AND FROMAGES BLANCS: this is a clever way of thickening *cuisine minceur* dishes, but these ingredients need a light touch – too much yogurt leaves a slightly sour taste and *fromage blanc* leaves an impression of dryness on the palate, which can only be overcome to a certain extent.

OTHER LIAISON METHODS: other liaisons can be achieved using specific 'blending agents' such as those produced from seaweed, or vegetable gums, like carob.

MARINADES

A method of soaking meat and game in an aromatic, spicy liquid, for a given period. In ancient times it was used as a way of preserving meat and enhancing its flavour.

Today, marinades are used primarly to tenderize and flavour meat, which must be kept in a cool place and turned frequently while it is marinating. The marinade is then often used as a cooking liquid, or as a base for an accompanying sauce. The benefits of marinating food in *cuisine minceur* are not insignificant. Marinades contain little or no fat, but as they both tenderize and flavour the food, this compensates for any richness that the dish may lack. To succeed with marinades in *cuisine minceur*, observe the following points:
• Thoroughly wipe the meat to be cooked to remove any fat or oil left from the marinade.

• If the marinade is to be used as a base for a sauce, refrigerate, then skim all the fat from the surface. Heat to evaporate the alcohol while retaining its aroma.

CLASSIC UNCOOKED MARINADE

1 onion
2 shallots
½ carrot
1 small celery stick, cut into thin strips
thyme
bay leaves
parsley
1 clove of garlic
2 cloves
6 peppercorns
6 grains of coriander
500 ml/17 fl oz white or red wine
10 tablespoons vinegar
6 tablespoons oil
pinch of salt

Make a bed with half the vegetables, herbs, garlic and spices on a flat dish. Put the meat on top and cover with the rest of the vegetables, herbs, garlic and spices. Sprinkle over the wine, vinegar, oil and seasonings.

COOKED MARINADE

This is prepared with the same ingredients, but speeds up the process of tenderizing the meat.

Soften the vegetables in a covered pan with the oil. Moisten with the wine and vinegar. Add the flavourings. Simmer for 30 minutes. Leave to cool before using as a marinade.

MARINADE MINCEUR

As they include little or no fat, marinades are invaluable in *cuisine minceur*.

The presence of spices, tenderizers and aromatic seasonings, allows the creation of a light dish without recourse to rich ingredients.

For their use in *cuisine minceur*:
• If the marinade contains a little oil, wipe the meat carefully before cooking.

• If the marinade is to be used as a basis for an accompanying sauce, skim off the fat, then reduce the liquid and evaporate the alcohol by heating, to retain just the aroma.

INFUSION: THE PERFECT MARINADE FOR *CUISINE MINCEUR*

The wine which is the basis of a marinade can be cleverly replaced by a 'spice bath': an infusion of water in which aromatic seasonings such as rosemary, marjoram and pistou have been boiled. The strained water should be cooled before use. The same infusion can be used to give an aromatic flavour when steaming certain white meats.

SAUCES

MAYONNAISE

Here is the classic recipe. A lighter version is given in the recipe on page 36. Mayonnaise is a cold emulsified sauce. The emulsion comes from the successful homogenous marriage of two ingredients which do not normally mix, for example water and an oily substance. Introducing a third foreign element, such as egg yolk or mustard, to the first two allows the union to take place.

Mayonnaise and its derivatives are all examples of a cold emulsified sauce, while sauces such as *Béarnaise*, *hollandaise* and others of their type, which unfortunately have no place in *cuisine minceur*, are all examples of a hot emulsified sauce.

1 egg
1 teaspoon Dijon-style mustard
salt
freshly ground white or cayenne pepper
175 ml/6 fl oz oil (groundnut, olive or other, depending on your taste)
few drops of vinegar (preferably wine vinegar) or lemon juice (better with olive oil)

Preparation time: 10 minutes

Separate the yolk from the egg white. Place the yolk in a bowl and add the mustard, salt and pepper (white pepper does not leave black specks in the sauce and is therefore preferable to black pepper).

Beat with a small whisk or wooden spoon. When the ingredients are well combined, pour the oil into the yolk mixture in a thin stream, beating smoothly and constantly. As the sauce thickens, add the vinegar or lemon juice a little at a time to thin it. Finish the mayonnaise by adding the rest of the oil and adjust the seasoning if necessary.

USEFUL TIPS: the egg yolk and oil should be at room temperature. If the mayonnaise curdles, mix it into a little mustard, little by little.

Keep the mayonnaise in a cool place but do not refrigerate: the oil might congeal and the sauce would separate.

USES: serve mayonnaise with fish and cold meats, or use it to bind vegetable or meat mixtures.

Mayonnaise takes on a new character when other ingredients are added to it. Here are some suggestions:
Aïoli: mayonnaise prepared with olive oil, garlic purée and cooked mashed potato.

The miniature range at the Guérard family home

The main central cooking stove at Les Prés d'Eugénie which was designed by Christine Guérard

Andalouse Sauce: mayonnaise, tomato purée and chopped sweet pepper.
Antiboise Sauce: mayonnaise prepared with olive oil, chopped coriander, chervil and parsley.
Sauce Vincent: mayonnaise, sorrel purée, chopped parsley, chervil, watercress, chives and hard-boiled eggs.
Tartar Sauce: mayonnaise, capers, chopped pickled gherkins (*cornichons*), onions, parsley, chervil and tarragon.
Wine Sauce: mayonnaise, red wine and shallots.

LIGHT MAYONNAISE

350 g/12 oz 0% fat fromage frais
2 tablespoons mustard
50 ml/2 fl oz red wine vinegar
salt and pepper
100 ml/3½ fl oz olive oil

Preparation time: 3 minutes

Place the *fromage frais*, mustard, vinegar, salt and pepper in a bowl and mix well. Add the oil in a very thin stream, beating constantly with a whisk, until the sauce is smooth and thick.

Note: although it should be used immediately, this mayonnaise can be kept at room temperature for 24 hours, covered with cling film, if necessary. You can make an excellent seafood cocktail sauce by adding to it a little tomato ketchup and about 10 drops of Tabasco sauce. You can also simply add fresh chopped herbs, either one kind or a mixture.

LIGHT VINAIGRETTE

250 ml/8 fl oz water
25 g/1 oz cornflour
2 tablespoons cold water
150 ml/¼ pint red wine vinegar
2 tablespoons mustard
2 tablespoons olive oil (or other oil)
10 drops of Worcestershire sauce
1 teaspoon salt
20 turns of the pepper mill

Preparation time: 5 minutes
Cooking time: 5 minutes

TO PREPARE THE THICKENING AGENT: bring the water to the boil in a saucepan. Dissolve the cornflour in the 2 tablespoons cold water and add to the boiling water. Beat constantly for 2 minutes while the mixture boils. Remove the saucepan from the heat and leave to cool for 30 minutes.

TO FINISH THE VINAIGRETTE: pour the cornflour mixture into a food processor. Add the remaining ingredients and process for 20 seconds. Transfer the sauce to a bottle and keep at room temperature.

Note: this light vinaigrette will keep for 3-4 weeks, covered, in the refrigerator. Shake the bottle well before each use.

SAUCE AMÉRICAINE

SERVES 6

1 live lobster, about 750 g/1 ¾ lb
1 tablespoon olive oil
1 tablespoon groundnut oil
1 tablespoon chilled butter
2 shallots, 1 carrot, ½ onion, all cut into very small cubes
(this mixture is called a mirepoix*)*
1 clove of garlic, unpeeled and lightly crushed
1 bouquet garni, with a sprig of tarragon
salt and pepper
3 tablespoons Armagnac or Cognac
3 fresh tomatoes, coarsely chopped
1 tablespoon tomato purée
pinch of cayenne pepper
250 ml/8 fl oz white wine
250 ml/8 fl oz fish fumet (see page 32) or water

BINDING
50 g/2 oz butter, mixed with the roe and tomalley (green
substance) of the lobster
1 teaspoon plain flour (optional)

Preparation time: 20 minutes
Cooking time: 25-30 minutes

The lobster should be killed immediately before it is to be used: take a large knife and push its point firmly down through the cross mark at the centre of the head. The lobster will be killed instantly.

Separate the tail and claws from the body of the lobster. Crack them with the dull edge of a heavy knife so that extracting the meat is easier after cooking. Split the body in half lengthwise. Discard the head sac found at the back of the head. Remove the roe and tomalley (green substance) and set aside in a bowl.

Cut the tail crosswise into several pieces. Heat the oil and butter in a frying pan. Gently cook the shallots, carrot, onion, garlic and *bouquet garni* without browning. Remove with a slotted spoon, draining them to leave as much fat in the pan as

Guérard cooking lobster

possible. Add the cut-up lobster, seasoned with salt and pepper, and cook gently until the shell turns red. Add the Armagnac or Cognac and cover. The brandy should boil until reduced by three-quarters, giving its aroma to the lobster meat. Do not flame the brandy, since this might burn the small claws of the lobster and ruin the sauce with a bitter taste.

Cover the lobster with the *mirepoix*, chopped tomatoes and tomato purée, and season with salt, pepper and cayenne pepper. Pour in the white wine and the fish *fumet*. Cook, covered, for 10 minutes over a high heat.

Remove the lobster pieces (the lobster meat can be used later – in a salad, for example) and boil, uncovered, until the liquid is reduced by a third. Pass through a fine-mesh sieve into another saucepan. Add the binding ingredients (butter, roe, tomalley and flour), beating them in with a whisk. Boil for 2 more minutes. Transfer to a container for storage.

Note: this sauce can be a very useful element in *cuisine minceur*. As with the three great stocks, it can be prepared in advance, and preserved, either in sterilized jars in the refrigerator, or frozen. Made with lobster, it is expensive to prepare. You can replace the lobster with fresh crab to lower the price, adding the bones of sole or flounder as well as crayfish heads or other shellfish. Naturally, this is a makeshift version and will therefore not be as flavourful as the original.

FRESH TOMATO SAUCE

1.5 kg/3¼ lb ripe tomatoes
1 tablespoon olive oil
2 onions, chopped
1 clove of garlic, chopped
2 tablespoons fresh thyme
1 bay leaf
salt

Preparation time: 10 minutes
Cooking time: 20-25 minutes

TO PREPARE THE TOMATOES: dip the tomatoes in boiling water for 30 seconds. Peel, halve and seed. Cut each half into pieces and set aside in a bowl.

Rub the thyme between your fingers to release the leaves.

TO COOK THE SAUCE: heat the olive oil over a low heat in a large frying pan. Add the onions, garlic, thyme leaves and bay leaf. Cook very gently for 5 minutes.

Add the tomatoes and mix. Simmer over a medium heat, uncovered, for about 20 minutes, stirring occasionally with a wooden spoon to prevent sticking. The sauce should be reduced and thick.

Note: in the winter months, replace the fresh tomatoes with canned peeled tomatoes. They should be drained and seeded.

SPICES, HERBS AND FLAVOURINGS

They come from all corners of the earth, from nearby hills and kitchen gardens or in the cupboard to add to your dishes, whether sweet or salty, acidic or bitter, delicate and subtle or strong and with robust flavours.

They are an indispensable part of *cuisine minceur* – maybe even more so than in classic cooking – how else would we give such light dishes a truly rustic or exotic flavour.

FLAVOURINGS

Salt the only mineral condiment – coarse or fine, rock salt or sea salt, it is the universal seasoning.

Sugar in all its forms is an indispensable condiment for desserts and pastries. In this book it is nearly always replaced by Nutrasweet (aspartame) which provides the necessary sweetness for the end of a meal.

Lemon (lemon juice), and **Wine** or **Fruit Vinegar** are used to give an acidic flavour to dishes.

Wines and **Alcohol** greatly reduced by evaporation are transformed into pure aromatic 'extracts', accentuating their flavours and scents.

Garlic, **Spring Onion**, **Mustard**, **Horseradish**, **Radish**, **Leek**, **Onion** and **Shallot** can be considered as pungent, powerful condiments, to enhance the flavour of a rather insipid dish.

SPICES

Pepper – ground, whole, crushed, white or black, like its partner, salt, is used in almost all culinary preparations. To retain its fine aroma, it is best to add it at the end of the cooking process.

Paprika – a pepper extracted from pimento (capsicum). It is also called red pepper and it imparts a beautiful deep red colour to sauces. It is used in all so-called 'Hungarian' dishes.

Cayenne – another red pepper. In powdered form it can be used in addition to, or to replace, black or white pepper to give added piquancy.

Nutmeg and Mace – nutmeg is the kernel of the seed of the nutmeg tree, and mace is the dried outer covering or aril, of the seed. Nutmeg is grated, mace is used in powdered form. Use sparingly, as the flavour is quite robust. They are ideal flavourings for gratins, stuffings and marinades for *foie gras*.

Saffron – this is the pistils (stigma) of the saffron crocus. Dark orange in colour, its flavour has no comparison and it is an indispensable addition to fish soups and stews.

Clove – this is the dried flower of the clove tree. It is a

The herb garden at Les Prés d'Eugénie

powerful antiseptic as well as a highly flavoured spice. It must therefore, be used sparingly, generally pushed into an onion, to flavour stocks and marinades.

Coriander – can be used as seeds or fresh, like parsley. The seeds and leaves have a particular, powerful taste. It is often used in North African cuisine.

Ginger – a fresh root that must be peeled before use. It is much used in Asian cooking and has an irresistible, very particular and slightly earthy flavour.

Cinnamon – this comes from Asia either in powdered form or in little sticks of rolled bark. It has an exquisitely fine taste –

warm and peppery which blends well with sugar to add flavour to certain pastries and other sweet dishes.

Vanilla – everyone knows that this is a marvellous spice which no *pâtissier* can do without. Available as a powder, an extract or in pods – this last has the best keeping qualities.

Fine Herbs – who wouldn't like to have his own herb garden where he could just go and pick what he needs when he needs it. Failing that, it is best to buy fresh herbs which keep well in a sealed container in the refrigerator.

Bouquet Garni – an essential element of French cuisine. Classically composed of sprigs of parsley, thyme and bay

A selection of fresh herbs

leaves, to this can be added a small stick of celery, a sprig of tarragon, a basil leaf, and a little of what you like. The herbs are tied together in a little bunch and can be easily removed when the dish is finished.

Parsley – this is often used as a garnish. It can be found in two varieties:

– curly parsley, absolutely delicious when it is fried and a good accompaniment to a dish of little fried fish.

– flat-leaved parsley has a more powerful aroma and is best used as a flavouring.

Chervil – with its fine leaves and delicate flavour, this is mostly used in a combination with other herbs, but also in salads, soups and as a garnish.

Tarragon – its long narrow leaves have a particular and powerful flavour. Often used in a mixture of fine herbs, but also as a good seasoning for salads, omelettes and certain sauces, such as fresh tomato sauce (*coulis*) or *Béarnaise* sauce.

Basil – very highly flavoured, very Mediterranean, it must be used very sparingly, but how delicious it is!

It is used as an ingredient in a *pesto* or *pistou* for soups and pasta dishes.

Rosemary – a herb from the hills of Provence, it is almost an essence. Used as an infusion it is an invaluable ally in *cuisine minceur*. In classic cuisine it is best used sparingly, so as not to be overpowering, to flavour roasts and grills.

Marjoram – the Italians' oregano. An extremely fragrant plant, whose delicate aroma offers plenty of scope for *cuisine minceur*.

Mint – there are several varieties: wild mint, garden mint, peppermint. They have a very fresh flavour, and are very good for adding to, and decorating desserts.

Very much appreciated in Arab countries, they are also very useful as infusions for *cuisine minceur*.

In Britain, mint sauce is the traditional accompaniment to roast lamb. Its finely chopped leaves are also often sprinkled over boiled potatoes or carrots.

Thyme – another herb which grows wild on the stony Provence hills. It is used as an ingredient in a bouquet garni. It is strongly flavoured, so use only a sprig, not a bunch! Rub between your hands to let some of the leaves and flowers fall and use to flavour rabbit, roast pork or lamb.

Bay – this is the last ingredient in a bouquet garni. Very powerful, just half a leaf is sufficient. Note that it should not be left in any dish that is not to be consumed immediately since it is so strong.

Fennel, Aniseed, Dill – all these have a flavour of aniseed. Their fresh leaves or dried stems can equally be used to flavour fish dishes.

The bulb of a fennel plant is eaten raw like celery.

Sage – a strong, slightly bitter flavour which is not to everyone's taste, but goes well with broad beans, peas and pork.

Savory – its flavour and aroma are similar to thyme, and should therefore be used sparingly. It has the same uses as sage and thyme.

Cumin – this has a very particular, aromatic taste. Usually ground, it is a dominant ingredient of North African cuisine.

Caraway – seeds with pungent, characteristic flavour. They are delicious in bread rolls and certain cakes and go well with cabbage and carrots.

Juniper – used to flavour game and *sauerkraut* (*choucroûte*). Small sprigs of juniper are used in marinades for game dishes.

REMARKS

• Spices and condiments, fine herbs and aromatic flavourings should always be used with care and in carefully measured quantities.

• Excessive use brings an imbalance to a dish which is difficult to resolve.

• Heat enhances their flavour.

• They should only be used as a secondary flavour to enliven the dish they are seasoning, be it meat, poultry, game, fish, or vegetables.

• While many of these plants – lime, hyssop, rosemary, thyme, marjoram and mint, for instance – are used for medicinal purposes – they can equally be used to flavour food.

• For baking (*pâtisserie*), cocoa, coffee, vanilla, cinnamon and the zests of oranges and lemons are the most useful aromatic condiments.

The list in this chapter is by no means exhaustive, since many countries offer many other suitable plants.

COCKTAIL SNACKS

BASKET OF CRUDITÉS WITH A DIPPING SAUCE

These are simply young raw vegetables that vary according to the season – and your own taste. They are served with a light dipping sauce and should be attractively arranged in a basket or on a large platter. You can also add preserved or pickled vegetables. Below are some suggestions.

SERVES 4

RAW VEGETABLES
3-4 long, narrow carrots
¼ red pepper
¼ yellow pepper
½ fennel bulb
¼ cucumber
4 pale yellow celery hearts
12 spring onions
½ bunch of radishes
2 large cauliflower florets

PICKLED VEGETABLES
10 black olives
10 green olives
1 large, smooth-skinned gherkin
8-10 tiny gherkins

DIPPING SAUCE
2 tablespoons chopped chives
120 g/4½ oz 0% fat fromage frais
1-2 tablespoons Dijon-style mustard
1 scant tablespoon olive or sesame oil
few dashes of Worcestershire sauce, or to your taste
1-2 dashes of Tabasco sauce, or to your taste
celery salt
pepper
½ teaspoon curry powder

Preparation time: vegetables: 30 minutes; sauce: 5 minutes

TO PREPARE THE VEGETABLES: wash all the raw vegetables and peel where necessary. Cut the carrots, peppers, fennel and cucumber in small sticks. Cut the celery hearts in half. Trim the spring onions, leaving 5 cm/2 inches of green stem. Wash and trim the radishes, leaving a little bit of green stem. Separate the cauliflower florets into tiny florets.

Place the olives on 2 separate saucers. Cut the large gherkin into rounds or lengthwise into 5 sticks and place on a small plate with the drained tiny gherkins.

PRESENTATION: arrange all the vegetables attractively in a large basket. To make the sauce, combine all the ingredients well and pour into a small bowl. Place in the middle of the vegetables. Each guest can dip vegetables into the sauce.

CAVIAR SUSHI

SERVES 4

40 g/1 ½ oz Japanese rice (see note right)
¼ teaspoon rice vinegar (see note right)
1 sheet of nori (Japanese dried seaweed) (see note right)
50 g/2 oz caviar (Beluga, salmon caviar or trout caviar)
few sprigs of dill

Preparation time: 5 minutes
Cooking time: 16 minutes

TO COOK THE RICE: place the rice in a small saucepan. Add twice its volume of cold water. Cook, covered, over a very low heat, for 16 minutes. All the water should be absorbed by the rice by the end of the cooking time.

Caviar Sushi

When the rice is cooked, mix in the rice vinegar and transfer to a plate. Cover the rice with a damp piece of kitchen paper.

GARNISH AND PRESENTATION: when the rice is lukewarm, gently spread it over the sheet of *nori* and roll into a compact sausage shape. Slice the roll into 8 rounds. Garnish each round with the caviar and dill and serve immediately.

Note: These products are available from Japanese and Oriental food shops.

CHICKEN LIVER CANAPÉS

SERVES 4

1 onion
4 dried juniper berries
100 g/4 oz chicken livers
1 teaspoon olive oil
salt and pepper
dash of red wine vinegar
8 thin slices of French baguette

Preparation time: 5 minutes
Cooking time: 5 minutes

TO PREPARE THE CANAPÉS: peel and very finely chop the onion. Crush the juniper berries with the flat side of a large knife blade. Cut the livers into very small pieces.

TO COOK THE LIVERS: heat the oil in a nonstick frying pan. Add the onion and fry gently for 4 minutes. Add the livers and fry for 1 minute over a high heat. Add salt and pepper to taste. Add a dash of vinegar while gently tossing the mixture. Set aside on a plate.

PRESENTATION: toast the bread slices. Spread some of the chicken liver mixture on each slice and sprinkle with the crushed juniper berries. Serve.

POPCORN WITH ROSEMARY SALT

SERVES 4

50 g/2 oz popping corn
sprig of dried rosemary
1 teaspoon salt
1 teaspoon oil (optional)

Preparation time: 1 minute
Cooking time: 2-3 minutes

TO PREPARE THE ROSEMARY SALT: strip the rosemary leaves from the stem and place them in a mortar. Add the salt and pound with a pestle, incorporating the ingredients until well mixed. Set aside.

TO COOK THE POPCORN: heat the oil in a nonstick saucepan over a medium heat. Add the corn and heat, covered, shaking the pan constantly, until the corn has finished popping. Alternatively, if you have an electric popcorn machine, pop the corn with or without the oil, following the manufacturer's instructions.

PRESENTATION: place the popcorn in a dish and season by adding the rosemary salt whilst tossing the popcorn. Serve the popcorn hot.

POTATOES STUFFED WITH ANCHOVY PASTE

SERVES 4

4 potatoes, about 50 g/2 oz each

ANCHOVY PASTE
4 anchovy fillets in oil, well drained
100 g/4 oz 0% fat fromage frais
¼ clove of garlic, chopped
1 teaspoon olive oil
salt and pepper
2 tablespoons finely chopped chives

Preparation time: 3 minutes
Cooking time: 12-15 minutes

TO PREPARE AND COOK THE POTATOES: brush and wash the potatoes, cut them in half lengthwise and cut a thin slice off each convex side so that they don't tip. With a melon baller, make a hollow in each half. Place the potato halves in a saucepan of cold salted water to cover, bring to the boil and cook until tender but still firm.

TO PREPARE THE ANCHOVY PASTE: blot the anchovies dry on kitchen paper. Put the *fromage frais*, the anchovies cut into 2 or 3 pieces, the garlic, oil and salt and pepper in a food processor and process for 20 seconds. Transfer the paste to a bowl. Add the chives and mix well.

PRESENTATION: when the potatoes are cooked, drain them and allow them to cool for 5 minutes. Fill each half with the anchovy paste. Serve warm.

SOUPS

ICED TOMATO AND BASIL SOUP WITH PIQUANT AVOCADO CROÛTONS

SERVES 4

SOUP

1 kg/2¼ lb very ripe tomatoes (or 1 large can tomatoes)
2 onions
1 clove of garlic
1 celery stick
bunch of basil
1 tablespoon olive oil
1 bouquet garni
500 ml/17 fl oz water
1 teaspoon Worcestershire sauce
salt and pepper

CROÛTONS

12 thin slices of French bread (baguette)
½ avocado
juice of 1 lime
¼ teaspoon Tabasco sauce
salt and pepper

Preparation time: 15 minutes, plus 2 hours resting
Cooking time: 15 minutes

TO PREPARE THE SOUP: plunge the tomatoes for 30 seconds into boiling water, then peel and seed them. Pour off any water from the tomatoes and cut them into quarters. (If using canned tomatoes, pour off the juice, seed and quarter.)

Peel the onions and garlic and chop finely. Remove any tough fibres from the celery, and chop very finely. Remove the leaves from the basil, discarding the stalks.

TO COOK THE SOUP: heat the olive oil in a medium saucepan. Add the garlic, onion, celery and bouquet garni. Mix together and leave to soften, covered, over a low heat for 5 minutes.

Add the tomatoes, water and half the basil leaves. Bring to the boil and cook over a high heat for 5 minutes.

Pour the soup into a blender, and switch on for 1 minute. Pass through a fine sieve into a salad bowl, pressing down with a small ladle to extract all the juice.

Leave to cool at room temperature, then refrigerate for 1½ hours.

TO PREPARE THE CROÛTONS: lightly grill the slices of French bread.

Remove the avocado from its skin with a spoon. Mash in a bowl with a fork to make a purée. Season with the lime juice, Tabasco and salt. Mix the purée well and spread on to the slices of toast.

FINISHING AND PRESENTATION: take the soup from the refrigerator. Add the Worcestershire sauce, check the seasoning and add salt and pepper, if necessary.

Put a ladleful of soup in the mixer. Add the remaining basil, reserving 4 leaves for garnish. Blend for 30 seconds, then stir back into the rest of the soup.

Divide the soup between 4 chilled soup plates. Add 2 or 3 ice cubes and a basil leaf to each plate. Serve the avocado croûtons separately.

CREAM OF PUMPKIN SOUP

SERVES 4

sprig of thyme
½ bay leaf
1 teaspoon oil
500 g/1 ¼ lb raw pumpkin flesh, finely chopped
1 onion, finely chopped
1 small clove of garlic, crushed
2 celery sticks, finely chopped
1.25 litres/2 ¼ pints poultry stock (see page 31)
salt and pepper
1 tablespoon skimmed milk powder
1 tablespoon 0% fat fromage frais
2 tablespoons chopped parsley, chervil and chives

Preparation time: 10-15 minutes
Cooking time: 30 minutes

PREPARATION: remove the leaves from the sprig of thyme and crush the ½ bay leaf into tiny pieces.

TO COOK THE SOUP: heat the oil in a saucepan over a low heat. Add the pumpkin, onion, garlic, celery, thyme and bay leaf. Sweat gently, covered, for 8 minutes, stirring occasionally. Add the poultry stock and simmer for 20 minutes.

TO FINISH THE SOUP: when the pumpkin is cooked, purée the soup in a food processor until it is smooth. Pass through a fine-mesh sieve into a saucepan.

Bring the soup to the boil. If it seems too thick, thin it with a little hot stock.

Transfer to a food processor once more and add salt and pepper. Add the milk powder and the *fromage frais*. Process for 20 seconds.

PRESENTATION: divide the pumpkin soup between 4 heated soup plates. Sprinkle with chopped fresh herbs and serve immediately.

LOW-FAT MINESTRONE WITH CHICKEN QUENELLES

SERVES 4

BROTH

1 carrot
1 leek
1 onion
1 turnip
1 celery stick
1 clove of garlic
1 level tablespoon chopped parsley
4 basil leaves, chopped
1 bouquet garni
1.5 litres/2 ¼ pints poultry stock (see page 31)

CHICKEN QUENELLES

120 g/4 ½ oz raw chicken breast
1 onion
2 tablespoons grated Parmesan cheese
1 tablespoon chopped parsley
½ clove of garlic
1 egg white
50 g/2 oz 0% fat fromage frais
salt and pepper

GARNISH

1 tablespoon chopped parsley
4 basil leaves, chopped

Preparation time: 15 minutes
Cooking time: broth: 15 minutes; quenelles: 5 minutes

TO PREPARE AND COOK THE BROTH: cut the vegetables into 1 cm/½ inch cubes. Put the herbs and vegetables in a saucepan. Add the bouquet garni and the poultry stock. Bring to the boil and cook over a low heat for 15 minutes.

TO PREPARE AND COOK THE CHICKEN QUENELLES: while the broth is cooking, cut the chicken and onion into pieces. Put them in a food processor with the remaining ingredients for the quenelles and process for 30 seconds, until puréed. Set aside.

When the broth is ready, lower the heat until it is barely simmering. With a teaspoon, form little balls of the chicken mixture. Drop them into the soup, pushing them gently from the spoon with your fingers. Poach for 5 minutes.

PRESENTATION: pour the soup into a well-heated soup tureen. Sprinkle with the chopped parsley and basil and serve immediately.

CREAM OF CARROT SOUP WITH FRESH THYME

SERVES 4

1 tablespoon olive oil
500 g/1¼ lb carrots, finely sliced
2 tablespoons thyme leaves
1 onion, finely sliced
½ clove of garlic, finely sliced
½ bay leaf
salt and pepper
1.25 litres/2¼ pints poultry stock (see page 31)
2 tablespoons skimmed milk powder
4 tablespoons chopped chervil or dill

Preparation time: 10 minutes
Cooking time: 20 minutes

TO COOK THE SOUP: heat the oil in a saucepan over a low heat. Add the carrots, onion, garlic, thyme, bay leaf, and salt and pepper. Cover and sweat gently for 8 minutes, stirring the vegetables occasionally.

Add the poultry stock and simmer, covered, for

10 minutes. Transfer to a food processor and process until creamy and smooth. Add the milk powder and process for 5 more seconds. Pass through a fine-mesh sieve into a saucepan and reheat gently. Adjust the seasoning. If the soup is too thick, thin with a little hot stock.

PRESENTATION: divide the soup between 4 very hot soup plates. Sprinkle with the chervil or dill. Serve immediately.

QUICK CHERVIL AND OAT FLAKE SOUP

SERVES 4

150 g/5 oz chervil
75 g/3 oz oat flakes
1.5 litres/2¾ pints poultry stock (see page 31)
salt

Preparation time: 5 minutes
Cooking time: 5 minutes

TO PREPARE AND COOK THE SOUP: wash and remove the stems from the chervil.

Bring the poultry stock to the boil; add the oat flakes and the chervil leaves. Cook over a high heat for 2 minutes.

Pour the soup into a food processor and process for 1-2 minutes, until the mixture is smooth and creamy.

Reheat the soup in a saucepan without boiling. Season with salt to taste. Pour into warm bowls and serve.

VARIATIONS: you may replace the chervil with watercress, spinach, or a mixture of all three. If you would like a creamier soup, you may add 2 tablespoons of skimmed milk powder when you process the soup.

LANGOUSTINE OR PRAWN BISQUE

SERVES 4

1 kg/2¼ lb langoustines or 750 g/1¾ lb large prawns

COURT BOUILLON
shells of the langoustines or prawns
1 leek
1 small carrot
1 celery stick
2 shallots
1 clove of garlic
1 tablespoon oil
1 tablespoon tomato purée
250 ml/8 fl oz white wine
1.75 litres/3 pints water
1 chicken stock cube
pinch of saffron
1 bouquet garni
salt and pepper

BISQUE
4 tablespoons cornflour
salt and pepper
4 tablespoons skimmed milk powder
¼ teaspoon Cognac
4 large basil leaves, chopped
1 teaspoon chopped tarragon
1 tablespoon chopped chives

Preparation time: 20-25 minutes
Cooking time: 1 hour 20 minutes

PREPARATION: peel and wash the vegetables for the court bouillon. Slice them coarsely.

Separate the heads from the tails of the langoustines or prawns. Peel the tails and set them aside in a tea towel. Crush the heads, claws (if langoustines are being used) and shells.

TO COOK THE COURT BOUILLON: heat the oil in a large, heavy saucepan over a medium heat. Add the crushed shells, heads and claws and fry them for 5 minutes, stirring constantly.

Add the vegetables and the tomato purée and cook for 5 more minutes over a high heat, stirring well. Pour in the white wine, bring to the boil and boil for 30 seconds, scraping the bottom of the saucepan.

Add the water, the crushed stock cube, the saffron and the bouquet garni. Bring to the boil and simmer, covered, for 1 hour.

When the court bouillon has finished cooking, pass through a sieve over a large bowl, pressing hard on the shells and vegetables with the back of a ladle to extract all the flavour.

Pass through a fine-mesh sieve into a large saucepan to eliminate any remaining bits of shell and vegetables.

TO FINISH THE BISQUE: bring the court bouillon to the boil. Dissolve the cornflour with a little cold water and add to the saucepan. Bring back to the boil and boil for 4 minutes. Adjust the seasoning with salt and pepper. Reduce the heat until the bisque is barely simmering and add the langoustine or prawn tails. Poach for 3 minutes.

GARNISH AND PRESENTATION: with a slotted spoon, place the tails in 4 heated soup plates. Transfer the bisque to a food processor. Add the milk powder and the Cognac. Process for several seconds until smooth.

Pour the bisque over the tails. Sprinkle with the chopped herbs and serve immediately.

Note: you may substitute the same amount of lobster or crayfish for the langoustines.

Langoustine Bisque

SALADS

ARTICHOKE SALAD WITH FRESH PEAS

SERVES 4

4 cooked artichoke hearts (see page 127)
100 g/4 oz shelled fresh peas
1 bunch of fines herbes *(chives, flat-leaf parsley, tarragon,*
basil and spring onions)
4 bright-red round tomatoes
lemon juice
4 handfuls of mesclun *(see note right)*

VINAIGRETTE AND GARNISH
1 carrot
12 shelled walnut halves
1 tablespoon walnut oil
85 ml/3 fl oz light vinaigrette (see page 36)

Preparation time: 40 minutes

TO PREPARE THE SALAD AND GARNISH: wash, drain and remove the stems from the *fines herbes*. Set aside.

Peel and wash the carrot for the garnish. Julienne the carrot with the medium julienne disc of a food processor or with a sharp knife and then set aside in a bowl covered with cling film.

Coarsely grind 8 walnut halves in a food processor, reserving the other 4 halves.

TO PREPARE THE VINAIGRETTE: pour the walnut oil into the light vinaigrette and beat lightly.

GARNISH AND PRESENTATION: cut each tomato in 6 wedges, seed, and reserve only the outer crescent of the tomato. Trim the artichoke bottoms and cut each in 6 wedges, sprinkling each wedge with lemon juice to prevent it darkening.

Arrange 6 tomato wedges around the edge of each plate; place an artichoke wedge between each tomato wedge.

In a large bowl, toss together the *mesclun*, *fines herbes* and raw fresh peas. Add the vinaigrette and toss gently with your fingers. Place some salad in the centre of each plate. Sprinkle over the coarsely ground walnuts and the julienned carrot. Garnish each mound of salad with a walnut half.

Note: *mesclun* is a mixture of several varieties of small salad leaves. It is now available in speciality food shops. You can prepare your own *mesclun* by mixing together the hearts of any available lettuces (for example, escarole, lamb's lettuce, butterhead, radicchio and curly endive).

TENDER GIBLET SALAD WITH SWEET AND SOUR VEGETABLES

SERVES 4

500 g/1 ¼ lb chicken giblets (see note right)
small bouquet garni
1.5 litres/2 ¾ pints water
salt
100 g/4 oz carrots
100 g/4 oz celeriac or turnip
100 g/4 oz cooked beetroot

SEASONING
4 tablespoons red wine vinegar (in all)
2 scant teaspoons Nutrasweet sweetener
salt and pepper
1 tablespoon olive oil
2 tablespoons finely chopped onion

GARNISH
2 tablespoons chopped chives

Preparation time: 15-20 minutes
Cooking time: 1 ½ hours

TO PREPARE AND COOK THE GIBLETS: carefully clean the giblets. Place in a saucepan, with the bouquet garni, cover with the water, season with salt and bring to the boil. Simmer for 1½ hours.

TO PREPARE THE VEGETABLES: peel and wash the carrots and celeriac. Julienne with the medium julienne disc of a food processor or with a sharp knife. Peel the beetroot. With a small knife, cut the beetroot in the same size julienne as the other vegetables.

TO COOK THE VEGETABLES: in a saucepan, bring about 500 ml/17 fl oz of water to the boil. Add the julienned carrots and celeriac and cook for 1 minute. Drain carefully.

While the vegetables are still hot, season with half the wine vinegar, half the sweetener, and salt and pepper. Set aside.

Place the julienned beetroot in a small saucepan, and add 1 tablespoon vinegar, the remaining sweetener, and salt and pepper. Heat for 2-3 minutes, stirring gently, until the vinegar has evaporated.

GARNISH AND PRESENTATION: when the giblets are cooked, drain and dry them. Season with the remaining tablespoon of vinegar, the olive oil, chopped onion and pepper.

Arrange the giblets in the middle of 4 plates, surround with the julienned vegetables and sprinkle everything with the chopped chives. Serve.

Note: for a variation you can replace the giblets with the same quantity of chicken livers, cooking them as for Chicken Liver Canapés (see page 44).

CUCUMBER AND TOMATO SALAD WITH LIME AND MINT DRESSING

SERVES 4

2 small cucumbers
4 tomatoes

DRESSING
bunch of fresh mint
juice of 2 limes
200 ml/7 fl oz very low-fat natural yogurt
salt and pepper

Preparation time: 15 minutes

TO PREPARE THE SALAD: wash and peel the cucumbers, cut a slice off each end and halve lengthwise. With a teaspoon, scrape out the seeds and cut each half into 5 mm/¼ inch slices.

Wash the tomatoes, cut out the stem end and halve each tomato lengthwise. Remove the seeds and juice. (If you prefer peeled tomatoes, dip them for 30 seconds into boiling water, then into iced water. Peel them with a small knife.) Cut the tomatoes into 1 cm/½ inch cubes.

TO PREPARE THE DRESSING: wash the mint and remove the stems. Chop very coarsely.

Beat the lime juice into the natural yogurt; season with salt and pepper.

PRESENTATION: in a large bowl, gently toss the cubed tomatoes and sliced cucumbers with the lime and mint dressing. Serve the salad in a salad bowl or alternatively on 4 individual plates.

SALAD OF COD AÏOLI WITH TOMATO CONFIT

SERVES 4

175 g/6 oz cod, skin removed
25 g/1 oz tomato, seeded
25 g/1 oz courgette
40 g/1 ½ oz peeled potato
500 ml/17 fl oz milk (prepared with milk powder)
1 teaspoon coarse salt
1 clove of garlic
sprig of thyme
½ bay leaf

MAYONNAISE

1 egg yolk
1 teaspoon strong, Dijon-style mustard
1 teaspoon lemon juice
1 clove of garlic, finely chopped
1 tablespoon safflower oil
2 teaspoons chopped fines herbes

TOMATO CONFIT

1 tomato
salt and pepper
pinch of Nutrasweet sweetener
pinch of flowering thyme (or ordinary thyme)
1 clove of garlic, crushed
1 tablespoon olive oil

GARNISH

handful of lamb's lettuce
2 basil leaves

Preparation time: 15 minutes
Cooking time: cod: 6-8 minutes; tomato: 35 minutes

TO PREPARE THE TOMATO CONFIT: preheat the oven to 160°C/325°F/Gas Mark 3.

Dip the tomato into boiling water for 30 seconds. Peel, halve and squeeze each half gently to remove the juice and seeds.

Arrange the tomato halves in a small ovenproof dish and sprinkle with the salt, pepper and sweetener. Add the thyme and the crushed garlic. Sprinkle with the olive oil and bake in the oven for 35 minutes. Cool.

TO PREPARE AND COOK THE VEGETABLES: cut the tomato, courgette and potato into 5 mm/¼ inch cubes. Cook the courgette and potato until tender but firm, drain and reserve.

TO PREPARE THE MAYONNAISE: combine the egg yolk, mustard, lemon juice and garlic. Beat the oil into the mixture, drop by drop, to form a mayonnaise.

TO COOK THE COD: pour the milk into a saucepan, together with the salt, garlic, thyme and bay leaf. Heat until barely simmering, add the cod and cook for 6-8 minutes. Remove the fish with a slotted spoon and place on a tea towel to drain.

TO PREPARE THE COD AÏOLI: combine the mayonnaise, the reserved cubed vegetables and the chopped *fines herbes*. Flake the cod carefully, reserving several large flakes for garnishing each plate. Add the remaining flaked fish to the mayonnaise and vegetable mixture.

GARNISH AND PRESENTATION: arrange some cod *aïoli* (the fish and mayonnaise) on each plate in the form of a little cake. Arrange the reserved flaked fish on top. Surround the *aïoli* with lamb's lettuce and place a cooked tomato half on the other side of the plate; garnish it with a basil leaf.

MUSSEL SALAD WITH CRUNCHY SPINACH

SERVES 4

1.5 kg/3¼ lb mussels
350 g/12 oz young spinach

SAUCE
100 ml/3½ fl oz fish fumet (see page 32) or
poultry stock (see page 31)
100 ml/3½ fl oz white wine
1 tablespoon red wine vinegar
1 small shallot, chopped
pinch of saffron
sprig of thyme
salt and pepper
1 tablespoon 0% fat fromage frais
2 tablespoons chopped dill

GARNISH
1 tomato, seeded and cut into julienne strips

Preparation time: 30-35 minutes
Cooking time: 20 minutes

TO PREPARE THE SALAD: scrape and carefully wash the mussels in several changes of water. In an earthenware pot over a high heat, cook the mussels until they open (about 3-4 minutes), stirring them well. Discard any which do not open. Remove from the heat and leave to cool.

Remove the stalks from the spinach, wash under running water, drain and dry carefully on a tea towel.

Shell the mussels and set them aside in a bowl covered with cling film. Pass the mussel liquid through a fine-mesh sieve lined with a double layer of muslin set over a saucepan.

Reserve some of the spinach leaves for a garnish, if liked and carefully cut the remainder into very thin strips, about 5 mm/¼ inch wide. Arrange the strips of spinach in 4 mounds in the centre of 4 plates with the whole spinach leaves around them, if using.

TO PREPARE AND COOK THE SAUCE: combine the fish *fumet*, white wine, vinegar, shallot, saffron, thyme and mussel liquid and season with salt and pepper. Bring to the boil over a medium heat; reduce over a low heat.

GARNISH AND PRESENTATION: arrange the mussels around the spinach mounds on each plate. When the sauce has reduced to almost half (there should be about 250 ml/8 fl oz remaining), remove from the heat. Remove the sprig of thyme, beat in the *fromage frais* and add the chopped dill.

Pour the sauce over the mussels, sprinkle with the tomato and serve. Garnish with empty mussel shells if liked.

Note: before pouring the sauce over, you can put the plates in a hot oven for 1 minute to warm the spinach and mussels.

Mussel Salad with Crunchy Spinach

Curly Endive Salad with Chicken Livers and Cinnamon Apples

CURLY ENDIVE SALAD WITH CHICKEN LIVERS AND CINNAMON APPLES

SERVES 4

1 head of curly endive (frisée)
400 g/14 oz chicken livers
2 Granny Smith apples
2 pinches of powdered cinnamon
juice of 1 lemon
4 teaspoons olive oil
2 pinches of caster sugar
200 ml/7 fl oz poultry stock (see
page 31)
salt and pepper
1 small shallot, chopped
1 tablespoon red wine vinegar
2 tablespoons chopped parsley

Preparation time: 20 minutes
Cooking time: apples: 4-5 minutes; liver: 3-4 minutes

TO PREPARE THE SALAD: separate the leaves and carefully wash the curly endive, dividing it into 4 handfuls of small, pale yellow leaves.

Peel and core the apples; cut them into small cubes and sprinkle with the lemon juice. Remove any membrane from the livers.

TO COOK THE APPLES: in a large nonstick frying pan, heat 2 teaspoons of the olive oil over a high heat. When the oil is hot, add the apples, cinnamon and sugar and fry gently for 4-5 minutes, stirring constantly.

When the apples are golden brown on all sides, add the poultry stock and, with a spatula, gently scrape the bottom of the pan without crushing the apples. Allow to boil gently for 1 minute.

Set aside the apples and their cooking liquid on a plate.

PRESENTATION OF THE SALAD AND COOKING THE LIVERS: divide the curly endive, the apples and their cooking liquid between 4 warmed plates. Heat a frying pan over a high heat and pour in the remaining olive oil. As soon as it begins to smoke, add the livers, seasoned with salt and pepper, and fry them gently, turning them on all sides, for 3 minutes.

Add the chopped shallot and the vinegar to the pan, stir, and cook over a high heat for 30 seconds, scraping the bottom of the pan.

Put the livers and their juice over the salad on the 4 plates, sprinkle with the chopped parsley and serve immediately.

Notes: when the livers are cooked, they should be quite pink inside. After you remove them from the frying pan, you can leave them to stand for 2-3 minutes; they will become even more tender.

You may replace the apples with pears or mangoes, as long as they are not overly ripe.

You may also replace the chicken livers with a thick slice of calf's liver, making sure that it is rosy inside, when cooked. Allow it to stand for 5 minutes before cutting it into thin slices and arranging them on top of the salad.

WARM SCALLOP SALAD WITH CAVIAR AND MUSHROOMS

SERVES 4

12 shelled scallops
120 g/4 ½ oz mousserons (see note right)
120 g/4 ½ oz cooked artichoke hearts (see page 127)
250 ml/8 fl oz chicken stock (made with ½ stock cube)
2 white mushroom caps
dash of lemon juice
3 tablespoons olive oil
½ small clove of garlic, crushed
75 g/3 oz mesclun (mixed salad leaves)
1 tablespoon chopped fines herbes
salt and pepper

VINAIGRETTE
250 ml/8 fl oz water
25 g/1 oz cornflour
2 tablespoons cold water
150 ml/¼ pint red wine vinegar
2 tablespoons Dijon-style mustard
2 tablespoons olive oil
1 teaspoon salt
20 turns of the pepper mill
dash of Worcestershire sauce

GARNISH
20 g/¾ oz caviar
tiny sprigs of chervil, flat-leaf parsley and chives

Preparation time: about 45 minutes
Cooking time: vinaigrette: 5 minutes; mushrooms: 6-7
minutes; scallops: 1 minute

TO PREPARE THE VINAIGRETTE: bring the water to the boil, add the cornflour, dissolved in the 2 tablespoons cold water; beat vigorously, and boil for 2 minutes. Remove from the heat and leave to cool for 30 minutes.

Pour the mixture into a food processor, add the remaining ingredients and process for 20 seconds. Transfer to a bottle or jar and keep at room temperature.

TO PREPARE THE SCALLOPS: cut each scallop in half to obtain 2 rounds and reserve in a tea towel.

TO PREPARE AND COOK THE VEGETABLES: cut the artichoke hearts into 7.5 cm/3 inch cubes.

Trim the stems of the *mousserons*, wash carefully and cook for 6-7 minutes in the chicken stock; drain. Clean the white mushroom caps, cut them into small, thin sticks and drizzle with the lemon juice. Set aside. Pour 2 tablespoons of the olive oil into a hot nonstick frying pan and gently fry the *mousserons* until quite crisp. Add the artichoke cubes, combine and stir for a moment.

Place the mixture in a saucepan, add the crushed garlic and mix together. Keep warm.

PRESENTATION OF THE SALAD: arrange some *mesclun* seasoned with vinaigrette on each plate. Sprinkle some chervil, parsley and chives over the *mesclun*, as well as the white mushroom sticks. Add the tablespoon of chopped *fines herbes*, seasoned with vinaigrette, to the saucepan of *mousserons* and artichokes. Mix well and divide among the 4 plates, placing the mixture on one side of the salad.

TO COOK THE SCALLOPS: heat the remaining tablespoon of olive oil in a nonstick frying pan over a medium-high heat. Add the scallops and season with salt and pepper. Cook for 30 seconds on each side.

Arrange 6 pieces of scallop on each plate on top of the *mousseron* and artichoke mixture. With the tip of a knife, place a tiny mound of caviar on each scallop. Garnish with chervil sprigs and serve immediately.

Note: *mousserons* are small white or beige mushrooms with a delicate flavour, and are also known as millers or fairy ring mushrooms. As they are difficult to obtain, ordinary field mushrooms can be substituted.

SALAD FROM 'MAMY'S' GARDEN

SERVES 4

4 heads of chicory
3 red tomatoes
100 g/4 oz dwarf French beans
12 baby spring onions
12 miniature carrots
100 g/4 oz miniature turnips
100 g/4 oz tiny fresh broad beans, shelled, or 100 g/4 oz fresh
peas, shelled

DRESSING
6 tablespoons light vinaigrette (see page 36)
25 g/1 oz mixed chervil, tarragon, parsley and basil leaves

Preparation time: 35-40 minutes
Cooking time: 5 minutes

TO PREPARE THE SALAD: wash and dry the chicory heads. Cut 1 cm/½ inch off the base of each one, separate the leaves and reserve 36 of the nicest. Shred the remaining leaves into 2.5 cm/1 inch lengths.

Remove the stems from the tomatoes. Quarter each tomato, seed each quarter and cut into 3 sections. Set aside.

String the French beans, wash and reserve. Peel and wash the onions, carrots and turnips, leaving about 2.5 cm/1 inch green stem; set aside. Dip the broad beans in boiling water for 30 seconds, slip off their outer skin and set aside.

TO COOK THE VEGETABLES: put the turnips, carrots and onions in a saucepan of salted boiling water. Cook for 3-4 minutes from the moment the water returns to the boil. Remove the vegetables with a slotted spoon, refresh in cold water and drain.

Put the French beans into a saucepan of salted boiling water; cook for about 5-6 minutes from the moment the water returns to the boil. The beans should stay firm. Refresh in cold water and drain.

GARNISH AND PRESENTATION: arrange 9 of the reserved chicory leaves and 9 tomato strips on each plate, alternating them around the edge. In a large bowl, combine the shredded chicory, French beans and broad beans and season with 3 tablespoons of the light vinaigrette. Arrange these vegetables attractively in the centre of each plate.

Season the remaining vegetables with the remaining vinaigrette. Arrange the turnips, onions and carrots on each chicory leaf, dividing the vegetables equally between the plates. Sprinkle the salads with the *fines herbes* and serve.

Salad from 'Mamy's' Garden

COLD STARTERS

RIPE TOMATO BAVAROIS
WITH FENNEL SALAD

SERVES 4

2 tablespoons powdered gelatine
300 g/11 oz well-reduced fresh tomato sauce (see page 38)
300 g/11 oz 0% fat fromage frais
2 tablespoons chopped basil
salt and pepper

SALAD

1 large or 2 small fennel bulbs
1 tablespoon chopped basil
1 tablespoon olive oil
1 tablespoon red wine vinegar
salt and pepper
6 black olives
sprigs of dill
3 ripe tomatoes, seeded, peeled and quartered (optional)

Preparation time: 20 minutes, 1 ½ hours in advance

TO PREPARE THE BAVAROIS: dissolve the gelatine in 2 tablespoons cold water and add to the hot tomato sauce. Heat, stirring constantly, over a low heat for 1 minute. Pour into a food processor and process until puréed. Add the *fromage frais* and chopped basil, season with salt and pepper and process for 20 seconds more.

Fill 4 small ramekins with the mixture, tapping each on the work surface to pack down the mixture and to make sure each ramekin holds the same amount. Refrigerate for 1½ hours.

TO PREPARE THE SALAD: cut the green stems and leaves off the fennel bulbs. Trim 5 mm/¼ inch off the hard bottoms. Slice the bulbs very finely. Add the basil to the fennel.

In a cup, make the dressing by mixing the oil, vinegar, salt and pepper. Pour over the fennel and basil and toss gently.

GARNISH AND PRESENTATION: divide the fennel salad between 4 plates. Unmould a bavarois on top of each one. Stone the black olives and top each bavarois with an olive half. Slice the remaining olives into strips and surround the bavarois and fennel salad with them. Sprinkle with sprigs of dill, then serve immediately. Garnish the dish with peeled ripe tomato quarters, if liked.

STUFFED TOMATOES
À L'OSTENDAISE

SERVES 4

4 tomatoes, about 100 g/4 oz each
150 g/5 oz cooked tiny grey shrimps
4 hard-boiled egg whites
2 tablespoons 0% fat fromage frais
2 tablespoons tomato ketchup
1 tablespoon olive oil
1 tablespoon chopped onion
1 tablespoon chopped parsley
1 tablespoon chopped tarragon
juice of ¼ lemon
salt and pepper

Preparation time: 20 minutes

PREPARATION: dip the tomatoes into boiling water for 30 seconds. Peel and cut the top off each one. With a spoon, scrape out the insides. Place the tomatoes cut side down on a plate so that the juice runs out.

Peel the shrimps and set aside the tails.

PRESENTATION: mash the egg whites with a fork. Add the *fromage frais*, shrimps (reserving a few for garnish) and all the remaining ingredients. Combine well.

Stuff the tomatoes with the shrimp mixture. Replace the tops and refrigerate for a short time. Serve on a platter or on individual plates.

Note: the tomatoes can be stuffed with crab, lobster, leftover poached fish, ham or leftover roast veal.

CHICKEN LIVER TERRINE
WITH APPLES

SERVES 4

250 g/9 oz raw chicken breasts, skin removed
3 egg whites
salt and pepper
pinch of allspice
150 ml/¼ pint chicken stock, prepared with a stock cube
1 tablespoon Calvados
1 teaspoon olive oil
1 clove of garlic, chopped
2 onions, chopped
2 tablespoons port
100 g/4 oz dried apple slices
500 g/1 ¼ lb chicken livers
sprig of thyme
1 bay leaf

GARNISH
1 tablespoon powdered gelatine
175 ml/6 fl oz boiling water
1 tablespoon Calvados

ACCOMPANIMENT
tiny pickled gherkins in vinegar, or raw apple salad dressed
with lime juice and curry powder

Preparation time: 30-35 minutes, at least 1 day in advance
Cooking time: 50 minutes

TO PREPARE THE TERRINE: cut the chicken breasts into cubes. Put them in the freezer for 5 minutes.

Place the chicken breasts in a food processor. Process at high speed for 20 seconds until finely minced. Add the egg whites, salt, pepper and allspice; process for 20 seconds more at high speed. Scrape the sides of the processor bowl, bringing the mixture towards the centre, pour in half the stock and the Calvados and process for 25 seconds more. Add the remaining stock and process for 30 seconds. Transfer the mixture to a large bowl and refrigerate.

Heat the olive oil over a medium heat in a frying pan. Add the garlic and onions and fry gently for 5 minutes then remove from the pan. Add the port to the pan and deglaze. Once reduced remove from the heat and set aside.

Cut the dried apple slices into small sticks and set aside.

Coarsely chop the chicken livers by processing for 5 seconds or by using a large knife. Remove the chicken mixture from the refrigerator. Add the dried apples, chicken livers, onion and garlic mixture, deglazed mixture, thyme (rubbed between your fingers), bay leaf (crushed into tiny pieces), 2 pinches of salt, and 20 turns of the pepper mill. Mix all the ingredients gently to obtain a smooth mixture.

TO COOK THE TERRINE: preheat the oven to 190°C/375°F/Gas Mark 4.

Transfer the chicken mixture to a nonstick loaf tin. Tap the tin on the work surface to level out the mixture, then put it in the oven. After 20 minutes, reduce the heat to 160°C/325°F/Gas Mark 3 and cook for 30 minutes more. If the top browns too quickly, cover it with foil.

While the terrine is cooking, dissolve the gelatine in 1½ tablespoons cold water. Add the boiling water, mix well and add the Calvados. Cool to room temperature.

Remove the terrine from the oven and pour the gelatine over it. Leave to cool for 2 hours at room temperature, then refrigerate for 1-2 days.

PRESENTATION: cut 2 cm/¾ inch slices of terrine and place on individual serving plates; serve with the pickled gherkins or dressed apple salad.

STUFFED VEGETABLES WITH
TOMATO VINAIGRETTE

SERVES 4

4 small tomatoes (ripe and with their stalks intact)
4 small courgettes
4 small green peppers
salt and pepper

VEGETABLE STUFFING

2 tablespoons chopped white mushrooms in 5 mm/¼ inch cubes

1 tablespoon chopped skinned tomato

2 tablespoons chopped French beans

2 tablespoons chopped courgette

1 tablespoon chopped celeriac

1 tablespoon chopped herbs (chervil, chives, parsley and tarragon)

MAYONNAISE

1 egg yolk

1 teaspoon Dijon-style mustard

salt and white pepper

1 tablespoon olive oil

4 tablespoons groundnut oil

1 teaspoon lemon juice

2 tablespoons 0% fat fromage frais

TOMATO VINAIGRETTE

300 g/11 oz tomatoes

1 teaspoon tomato purée

1 shallot, chopped

1 tablespoon olive oil

3 tablespoons groundnut oil

1 tablespoon red wine vinegar

1 tablespoon lemon juice

salt and white pepper

GARNISH

4 basil leaves

4 sprigs of rosemary

4 sprigs of thyme

tiny sprigs of chervil

Preparation time: 1 hour

Cooking time: about 10 minutes

TO PREPARE THE VEGETABLES: cut around the stalk of each tomato with a small knife to mark out a 'lid'. Plunge the tomatoes into a pan of boiling water for 30 seconds, remove and refresh under iced water; drain. Peel each tomato,

except for the skin of the 'lid' surrounding the stalk. Then cut off the 'lids' and set aside. Scoop out the insides of the tomatoes with a small teaspoon and set aside, upside down.

Cook the courgettes in salted boiling water for 3-4 minutes, refresh under iced water and drain. Cut off a 'lid' from each one and hollow out the courgettes. Set aside.

Blanch the peppers for 1 minute in the same water as the courgettes, then refresh. Cut an oval 'lid' from the length of each pepper, remove the seeds and set aside.

TO COOK THE VEGETABLE STUFFING: do not cook the chopped mushroom and tomato.

Cook, separately, in salted boiling water, the French beans, courgettes and celeriac, then refresh under iced water. Drain well on a tea towel.

TO PREPARE THE MAYONNAISE AND FINISH THE STUFFING: put the egg yolk in a bowl, add the mustard, salt and white pepper. Beat with a small whisk. Pour in the oils in a thin stream, continuing to beat the mixture as it thickens. Add the lemon juice drop by drop to thin the mayonnaise, then add the rest of the oil. Mix in the *fromage frais* and season.

Add all the chopped vegetables and the chopped herbs to the mayonnaise. Gently mix with a spoon to combine.

TO STUFF THE VEGETABLES: sprinkle the interiors of the vegetables with salt and pepper and stuff with the vegetable and mayonnaise mixture. Set aside in the refrigerator.

TO PREPARE THE TOMATO VINAIGRETTE: cut away the stalks from the tomatoes, cut each tomato in 4 and purée in a food processor with the shallot. Pass through a fine-mesh sieve to remove the skin and seeds.

Pour the purée into a bowl and add the tomato purée, olive oil, groundnut oil, vinegar and, finally, the lemon juice, stirring constantly with a small whisk. Season with salt and pepper.

PRESENTATION: using a small ladle, cover 4 plates with the tomato vinaigrette and arrange on each one a stuffed tomato, courgette and green pepper in a triangle, placing the 'lids' next to the appropriate vegetable. Garnish with the basil leaves, sprigs of rosemary, thyme and a few sprigs of chervil.

RABBIT RILLETTES WITH GREEN PEPPERCORNS

SERVES 4

forequarters of a young rabbit, or 500 g/1 ¼ lb rabbit thighs
1 tablespoon olive oil
4 onions, chopped
4 cloves of garlic, peeled
1 bouquet garni
2 small sprigs of rosemary
salt and pepper
250 ml/8 fl oz water
120 ml/4 fl oz dry white wine
1 tablespoon green peppercorns

ACCOMPANIMENTS
4 thin slices of French country bread, toasted
green salad

Preparation time: 20 minutes, 12 hours in advance
Cooking time: 1 ½ hours

TO PREPARE THE RABBIT: cut the rabbit into 6 pieces.

Heat the oil over a medium heat in a stockpot. Add the onions and the whole cloves of garlic. Fry gently for 5 minutes. Add the rabbit pieces, bouquet garni, rosemary, salt and pepper. Add the water and the wine. Bring to the boil for a moment, then reduce the heat to very low, cover with a sheet of foil, place the lid on the pan and simmer for 1½ hours. Check regularly to make sure the stew is not sticking to the bottom of the pot. Add a little more water if necessary.

TO PREPARE THE RILLETTES: when the stew is cooked, remove the bouquet garni and rosemary and leave to cool for 30 minutes. Remove the pieces of rabbit and, with a small, pointed knife, cut the meat from the bones.

Place the meat, onions, garlic and cooking liquid on a plate; mash and mix the ingredients together with a fork. Crush the green peppercorns with the blade of a large knife and add to the rabbit mixture. Mix them in well and correct the seasoning with salt.

PRESENTATION: fill a ceramic jar or terrine with the rillettes. Tamp the mixture down and place in the refrigerator, at least overnight (it will keep for 4-5 days). Serve directly from the jar or terrine, accompanied by the toasted bread and a salad.

BEEF CARPACCIO WITH BASIL SAUCE

SERVES 4

250 g/9 oz very lean fillet steak

SAUCE
bunch of basil
2 tablespoons olive oil
½ clove of garlic (optional)
salt and pepper

ACCOMPANIMENT
1 green or mixed salad, as desired

Preparation time: 12 minutes

TO PREPARE THE BEEF: cut the beef in extremely thin slices or have your butcher cut it (possibly with an electric meat slicer).

TO PREPARE THE BASIL SAUCE: remove the stems from the basil, wash and snip off the leaves, dry and chop coarsely. Put the basil, olive oil, garlic cut in 2 or 3 pieces, and salt and pepper in a mini food processor. Process with a start-and-stop rhythm until well pureéd.

PRESENTATION: arrange the slices of beef so that they completely cover each plate. With a small brush, lightly and evenly spread the basil sauce over the meat. Serve with your choice of salad.

Note: you can serve the carpaccio as a main course by increasing the quantity of meat by about 200 g/7 oz and doubling the quantity of basil sauce.

Beef Carpaccio with Basil Sauce

DUO OF SEAFOOD TARTARS

SERVES 4

175 g/6 oz salmon fillet, bones and skin removed
175 g/6 oz cod fillet, bones and skin removed
8 tablespoons chopped parsley
2 tablespoons chopped chives

SAUCE
50 g/2 oz 0% fat fromage frais
1 tablespoon strong Dijon-style mustard
1 tablespoon olive oil
2 teaspoons Worcestershire sauce
salt and pepper

GARNISH
1 lime
1 lemon
8 tiny sprigs of chervil
8 tiny sprigs of dill

ACCOMPANIMENT
4 puffed rice cakes

Preparation time: 30 minutes

TO PREPARE THE FISH AND THE SAUCE: cut the salmon and the cod into 3 mm/⅛ inch cubes. Set aside separately.

In a large bowl, using a whisk, beat together all the ingredients for the sauce. Divide the sauce in half and pour into 2 containers. Place the salmon in one and the cod in the other. Mix each thoroughly. Adjust the seasoning with salt and pepper.

Divide the salmon mixture in half and place in bowls. Add half the chopped parsley to one and half the chopped chives to the other. Mix well to incorporate the herbs.

Repeat this step for the cod so that you have one cod mixture with parsley and one with chives.

GARNISH AND PRESENTATION: slice the lime and lemon crosswise and set aside.

With a tablespoon, make small quenelles (oval-shaped mounds) of the fish mixtures. You will need 8 of the salmon (4 with parsley, 4 with chives) and 8 of the cod (4 with parsley, 4 with chives). Arrange 4 quenelles on each of 4 chilled plates: 2 of salmon, each with a different herb, and 2 of cod, each with a different herb.

Place the lemon and lime slices between each quenelle, and garnish with a few sprigs of chervil and dill. Accompany this dish with puffed rice cakes; they are lighter than toast.

ARTICHOKE MOUSSE WITH GREEN VEGETABLE GARNISH

SERVES 8

ARTICHOKE MOUSSE
500 g/1 ¼ lb cooked artichoke hearts (see page 127 – reserve large leaves for garnish)
120 ml/4 fl oz double cream
3 tablespoons powdered gelatine
120 g/4 ½ oz 0% fat fromage frais
salt and pepper

GREEN VEGETABLE GARNISH
40 g/1 ½ oz fresh (or frozen) peas
10 small young leeks
20 small green asparagus spears

BRAISED VEGETABLES
250 g/9 oz fennel bulb
450 g/1 lb white mushrooms
16 baby spring onions
1 onion
1 carrot
2 tablespoons olive oil
sprig of thyme
½ bay leaf
2 cloves of garlic
salt and pepper
100 ml/3 ½ fl oz dry white wine
1 basil leaf

VINAIGRETTE
120 ml/4 fl oz cooking liquid from the braised vegetables
25 ml/1 fl oz sherry vinegar
juice of ½ lemon
25 ml/1 fl oz olive oil
2 pinches of celery salt
2 pinches of cayenne pepper
dash of Tabasco sauce
10 coriander seeds, crushed
salt and pepper

GARNISH
several of the nicest artichoke leaves
16 orange segments, peeled (see page 149)
8 grapefruit segments, peeled (see page 149)
sprigs of fresh herbs (for example, chervil, basil,
chives and tarragon)

Preparation time: 1 hour
Cooking time: 25 minutes

TO PREPARE THE ARTICHOKE MOUSSE: process the artichoke hearts in a food processor until well puréed. With a whisk, whip the double cream in a chilled bowl until it holds stiff peaks. Set aside in the refrigerator.

Dissolve the gelatine in 4 tablespoons cold water. Heat 4 tablespoons of the artichoke purée in a small saucepan, stirring constantly. Add the gelatine, mix well with a whisk and add the mixture to the remaining artichoke purée.

Using a wooden spoon fold the *fromage frais* into the artichoke purée , carefully fold in the whipped cream. Season with salt and pepper.

On a baking sheet, place 8 stainless steel flan rings, measuring 2.5 cm/1 inch high and 6 cm/2½ inches in diameter. Fill each with the artichoke mousse, smoothing the tops with a spatula. Set aside in the refrigerator.

TO PREPARE AND COOK THE GREEN VEGETABLES: shell the peas, peel and wash the leeks and trim them to about 13 cm/ 5 inches long. Peel the asparagus with a vegetable peeler. Cook each vegetable separately in salted boiling water. After cooking, refresh in iced water and place each type of

vegetable on a separate tea towel.

TO PREPARE AND COOK THE BRAISED VEGETABLES: halve the fennel bulb lengthwise and cut each half in 4; remove the hard stem end, which would remain hard after cooking. Clean and wash the mushrooms, dry with a tea towel and cut each into 4. Trim and peel the spring onions.

Peel and finely slice the onion and carrot. Heat the olive oil in a heavy-bottomed cast-iron stockpot. Gently fry the onion and carrot until soft and golden. Add the fennel and spring onions to the stockpot. Add the thyme, ½ bay leaf and the unpeeled cloves of garlic. Season with salt and pepper. Add the white wine and enough water to just cover the vegetables.

Simmer gently for 15 minutes over a medium heat, then add the mushrooms and the basil leaf. Raise the heat to finish cooking the mixture; the liquid should be greatly reduced. Remove from the heat and correct the seasoning. Transfer the mushrooms, spring onions and fennel to a dish. Discard the thyme and bay leaf.

TO PREPARE THE VINAIGRETTE: put 120 ml/4 fl oz cooking liquid from the braised vegetables in a food processor. Process for 5 seconds. Add the remaining ingredients for the vinaigrette and process for 15 seconds more. Set the vinaigrette aside in a bowl.

GARNISH AND PRESENTATION: place the reserved artichoke leaves in salted boiling water for 2 minutes, refresh under cold water and drain.

Place an artichoke mousse on one side of each plate (preferably white). (To remove the rings, slide the blade of a small knife round the inside of each one.) Garnish the mousses by surrounding them with the artichoke leaves.

On the opposite side of each plate, arrange the braised vegetables, the green vegetables and the citrus segments in a half circle. Drizzle the vegetables with the vinaigrette and sprinkle with tiny sprigs of fresh herbs.

LANGOUSTINE TAILS IN FRESH TOMATOES WITH TWO CAVIARS

SERVES 4

12 langoustine (or large prawn) tails
3 large tomatoes
15 g/½ oz black caviar
15 g/½ oz salmon caviar
8 Queen scallop shells
salt and pepper

HERB MAYONNAISE
1 egg yolk
1 teaspoon Dijon-style mustard
salt and pepper
2 tablespoons olive oil
1 tablespoon safflower oil (optional)
1 teaspoon lemon juice
dash of pastis (Ricard)
2 tablespoons chopped fines herbes *(fresh parsley, tarragon and basil)*

GARNISH
2 eggs
¼ onion, finely chopped
1 teaspoon chopped chives
tiny sprigs of chervil
tiny sprigs of parsley
tiny sprigs of tarragon
10 fresh coriander leaves
dash of lemon juice

Preparation time: 30-35 minutes
Cooking time: 4 minutes

TO PREPARE AND COOK THE LANGOUSTINES (OR PRAWNS): separate the heads from the tails. Shell the tails and season with salt and pepper.

In a very hot nonstick frying pan, cook the tails on both sides, turning them frequently. Remove from the pan and leave to cool.

TO PREPARE THE HERB MAYONNAISE: combine the egg yolk, mustard, salt and pepper in a bowl. Pour in the oil(s) in a thin stream, beating constantly, and add a little of the lemon juice from time to time. When the mayonnaise has emulsified, mix in the dash of pastis and the chopped herbs. Correct the seasoning with salt and pepper.

TO PREPARE THE TOMATOES: dip the tomatoes into boiling water for 30 seconds, then peel them. Quarter each tomato and, with a flexible knife blade, seed and remove the interior, leaving only a flat surface. Spread each flat wedge with the herb mayonnaise, top with a langoustine (or prawn) tail and roll up carefully. Set aside.

TO PREPARE THE GARNISH: beat the eggs in a small, nonstick pan and scramble by stirring constantly over a very low heat so they are smooth and creamy. Remove from the heat, transfer to a bowl and cool. Mix in the onion and chives.

PRESENTATION: arrange 3 tomato rolls in a half-circle on one side of each plate. Sprinkle liberally with tiny sprigs of chervil, parsley and tarragon and with the coriander leaves.

Fill each scallop shell with a spoonful of scrambled egg. In the centre of the egg mixture, place a little of each caviar.

Place 2 scallop shells on each plate opposite the tomato rolls. Drizzle everything with the lemon juice. Serve the herb mayonnaise separately in a sauceboat.

FRESH TUNA SASHIMI WITH SOY MARINADE

SERVES 4

350 g/12 oz fresh tuna in one piece, without skin or bones

MARINADE
4 tablespoons soy sauce
4 tablespoons red wine vinegar
2 tablespoons sesame oil
10 g/¼ oz fresh root ginger, chopped
2 basil leaves

Fresh Tuna Sashimi with Soy Marinade

GARNISH
100 ml/3½ fl oz water
salt
20 g/¾ oz Japanese-style glutinous rice
10 g/¼ oz black Japanese seaweed (nori)
1 tomato
½ bunch of chives, chopped

Preparation time: 20-25 minutes
Cooking time: rice: 16 minutes; seaweed: 1 minute

TO PREPARE THE GARNISH: put the water, salt and rice in a saucepan. Bring to the boil, cover and simmer for 16 minutes. Remove from the heat and set aside.

Put the seaweed in a saucepan and cover with cold water. Bring to the boil and boil for 1 minute. Drain and set aside.

Plunge the tomato into boiling water for 30 seconds, then peel. Quarter the tomato, remove the insides and cut each section into thin strips. Set aside.

TO PREPARE THE TUNA: cut in paper-thin slices. Divide the tuna slices between 4 plates, covering each plate.

TO PREPARE THE MARINADE: place all the ingredients for the marinade in a food processor. Process for 15 seconds until emulsified.

GARNISH AND PRESENTATION: pour some marinade over the tuna on each plate and spread with the back of a spoon. With your fingers, make 4 tiny cones of lukewarm Japanese rice. Place a cone in the centre of each plate. Sprinkle the seaweed, tomato strips and chopped chives over the tuna. Serve.

Note: you can replace the tuna with fresh salmon or sea bass.

71

BOUILLABAISSE TERRINE EN GELÉE WITH NIÇOIS VEGETABLES

SERVES 4

1 large fennel bulb
2 courgettes
1 cooked artichoke heart (see page 127)
lemon juice
500 ml/17 fl oz fish fumet (see page 32 – add 3 tomatoes,
1 clove of garlic and 2 pinches of fennel seed to the basic
ingredients)
200 g/7 oz red mullet fillet
200 g/7 oz monkfish, sliced
6 tablespoons powdered gelatine
100 ml/3½ fl oz water
pinch of saffron
½ teaspoon pastis (Ricard)
2 tablespoons wine vinegar
1 clove of garlic, crushed
salt and pepper

SAUCE
100 ml/3½ fl oz fish fumet (see page 32)
100 g/4 oz 0% fat fromage frais
2 tablespoons wine vinegar
1 tablespoon olive oil
¼ clove of garlic
few drops of pastis (Ricard)
pinch of saffron
pinch of curry powder

Preparation time: 40-45 minutes, 12 hours in advance
Cooking time: 25 minutes

TO PREPARE THE VEGETABLES: remove and discard the hard outer layer and tiny leaves of the fennel bulb. Quarter the bulb lengthwise. Quarter the courgettes lengthwise. Trim the cooked artichoke heart, slice thinly and then sprinkle with lemon juice.

TO COOK THE JELLY: bring the fish *fumet* to a very gentle simmer in a pan over a low heat. Poach the red mullet fillets in the *fumet* for 2 minutes. Remove with a slotted spoon and drain on a cloth. Repeat for the sliced monkfish.

Bring the *fumet* to the boil, uncovered, over a high heat. Reduce by half.

Cook the fennel for 10 minutes in salted boiling water. Remove with a slotted spoon and drain on a tea towel. Cook the courgettes for 2 minutes in the same boiling water and drain on a tea towel.

Dissolve the gelatine in the cold water. When the *fumet* has reduced by half, add the dissolved gelatine, then season with the saffron, pastis, vinegar and crushed garlic. Heat, stirring constantly over a very low heat, for 2 minutes. Correct the seasoning with salt and pepper. Leave to cool for 15 minutes.

TO ASSEMBLE THE TERRINE: lightly oil a long, narrow terrine dish and line it with cling film, making sure the cling film folds over the sides of the dish.

Spread a layer of mixed vegetables on the bottom and cover with a layer of fish. Continue layering vegetables and fish, alternating colours and ingredients, until all have been used up.

Pour in the cooled (but not set) *fumet*. Fill to the brim. Refrigerate for 12 hours.

TO PREPARE THE SAUCE: reduce the 100 ml/3½ fl oz fish *fumet* until you have 2 tablespoons of syrupy liquid. Place in a food processor with the remaining ingredients and process for 15 seconds. Pour into a sauceboat.

PRESENTATION: unmould the terrine on to a platter and cut into 2 cm/¾ inch slices with an electric knife or a sharp knife dipped into hot water. Serve with the sauce and, if you wish, a green salad.

Bouillabaisse Terrine en Gelée with Niçois Vegetables

WARM AND HOT STARTERS

ASPARAGUS WITH RAVIGOTE SAUCE

SERVES 4

1.25 kg/2¾ lb asparagus (see note below)

VINAIGRETTE
1 shallot, finely chopped
50 ml/2 fl oz white wine vinegar
200 ml/7 fl oz very low-fat natural yogurt
1 tablespoon strong Dijon-style mustard
2 tablespoons safflower oil
1 tablespoon chopped parsley
1 tablespoon chopped chives
1 tablespoon chopped tarragon

GARNISH
handful of tiny sprigs of chervil
4 radishes, finely sliced

Preparation time: 20-25 minutes
Cooking time: 8-15 minutes, depending on size of asparagus

TO PREPARE THE ASPARAGUS: trim the tough bottoms of the asparagus spears so that they are of equal length. Peel with a vegetable peeler, placing them in cold water as you work.

Bring some salted water to the boil in a large stockpot. Add the asparagus spears and cook for 8-15 minutes, depending on their size. They should be quite firm and should not bend when they are picked up. Remove them with a slotted spoon and drain on a tea towel. Fold the tea towel over the asparagus to keep it warm.

TO PREPARE THE VINAIGRETTE: place the shallot and the vinegar in a small saucepan. Bring to the boil and cook for 2 minutes, until the shallot is soft. Remove from the heat and set aside.

In a bowl, mix the yogurt and the remaining ingredients for the vinaigrette with a small whisk. Then add the shallot and vinegar mixture. Set aside at room temperature.

GARNISH AND PRESENTATION: arrange the asparagus on individual plates. Drizzle some sauce over the ends of the asparagus, sprinkle with the chervil and a few radish slices.

Note: White asparagus can be replaced with thick green asparagus.

VARIATIONS:
Leeks: 1.5 kg/3¼ lb
Preparation time: 15-20 minutes
Cooking time: 10-20 minutes, depending on size
Cook the leeks in salted boiling water or steam them. Serve them lukewarm with the sauce.

Salsify: 1kg/2¼ lb
Preparation time: 30 minutes
Cooking time: 15 minutes
Cook the salsify in salted boiling water, adding 3 tablespoons vinegar to prevent darkening. Serve lukewarm with the sauce.

WILD MUSHROOM TARTS WITH ASPARAGUS TIPS

SERVES 4

500 g/1 ¼ lb medium green asparagus
65 g/2 ½ oz puff pastry (fresh or frozen)
tiny sprigs of chervil

MUSHROOM FILLING
500 g/1 ¼ lb very white mushrooms
25 g/1 oz mousserons or field mushrooms (see note on page 60)
50 g/2 oz fresh or dried morels
1 tablespoon lemon juice
25 g/1 oz skimmed milk powder
250 ml/8 fl oz water
salt and pepper
1 tablespoon olive oil
1 tablespoon chopped shallot
25 ml/1 fl oz port
½ teaspoon potato flour (dissolved in a little water)
½ egg yolk
25 g/1 oz 0% fat fromage frais

SAUCE FOR ASPARAGUS
2 tablespoons port
1 tablespoon double cream
85 ml/3 fl oz fresh poultry stock (see page 31) or the same quantity made from a stock cube and water
2 tablespoons 0% fat fromage frais

Preparation time: 35-40 minutes
Cooking time: about 30 minutes

TO PREPARE AND COOK THE MUSHROOM FILLING: trim the stalks of the white mushrooms and wash carefully. Quarter the mushrooms, sprinkle with the lemon juice and cook for 4-5 minutes in a saucepan with the skimmed milk powder dissolved in the water. Season with salt and pepper. Drain the mushrooms and process in a food processor until completely puréed.

Chop the other mushrooms very finely. Heat the olive oil in a nonstick frying pan, add the chopped shallot, the *mousserons* or field mushrooms and the morels. Fry briefly until just coloured. Deglaze with the port, and add the potato flour dissolved in water. Add the white mushroom purée and cook for 2 minutes, stirring constantly with a wooden spoon. Transfer the mixture to a bowl and cool. When cool, add the ½ egg yolk and the *fromage frais*.

TO PREPARE THE TARTS: roll out the puff pastry until quite thin and cut out 4 rounds 13 cm/5 inches in diameter. Place the rounds on a baking sheet and prick with a fork. Spread some of the mushroom mixture on each round, leaving a 5 mm/¼ inch border. Set aside in the refrigerator.

TO PREPARE AND COOK THE ASPARAGUS: peel the asparagus with a vegetable peeler. Cut the tips to measure 6 cm/2½ inch long, and slice the stems into 5 mm/½ inch pieces. Cook the tips in salted boiling water for about 5 minutes and the stems for about 9 minutes. Refresh immediately in iced water. Drain well on a tea towel.

TO PREPARE AND COOK THE SAUCE: bring the 2 tablespoons port to the boil in a small saucepan to evaporate the alcohol. Add the double cream and the poultry stock. Boil for 3 minutes, remove from the heat and add the *fromage frais*. Keep warm.

COOKING AND PRESENTATION: preheat the oven to 190°C/375°F/Gas Mark 5.

Place the baking sheet with the mushroom tarts in the oven. Bake for 15 minutes.

Remove the tarts from the oven and place on individual plates. Heat the asparagus stems and tips in the sauce. Arrange the asparagus over the tarts and pour a little sauce round. Garnish with the chervil sprigs.

SMOKED SALMON PAUPIETTES STUFFED WITH LANGOUSTINES

SERVES 4

4 large, thin slices smoked salmon, about 65 g/2 ½ oz each
12 good-sized raw langoustines (or large prawns)
1 teaspoon olive oil
salt and pepper
3 tablespoons chopped chives
1 tablespoon chopped tarragon

SALAD
1 tomato
handful of mesclun *(mixed salad leaves – see note on*
page 53)
1 tablespoon light vinaigrette (see page 36)

SAUCE
120 ml/4 fl oz very low-fat natural yogurt
1 tablespoon herb mustard
1 tablespoon olive oil
½ teaspoon Worcestershire sauce
juice of 1 lemon
salt and pepper

GARNISH
25 g/1 oz salmon or trout caviar
sprigs of dill

Preparation time: 30 minutes
Cooking time: 2 minutes

TO PREPARE THE SALAD: dip the tomato in boiling water for 30 seconds, peel, quarter and scoop out and discard the insides. Cut each tomato quarter into thin strips.

Combine the *mesclun* and the tomato strips and arrange on the side of 4 plates.

TO PREPARE AND COOK THE LANGOUSTINES: peel the langoustine (or prawn) tails. Heat the olive oil in a large frying pan over a high heat. Line up the shellfish tails, lightly seasoned with salt and pepper, in the pan and cook for 1 minute on each side. When they are cooked, add the chopped herbs, coat the tails with the herbs and remove them with a slotted spoon to a plate. Set aside.

TO PREPARE THE SAUCE: put all the ingredients for the sauce in a food processor and process for several seconds. If the mixture seems too thick, thin with a little water.

GARNISH AND PRESENTATION: spread out the smoked salmon slices on a work surface. Cut each langoustine (or prawn) tail in 3 or 4 pieces and divide them among the salmon slices, placing them in the centre of each slice.

Tightly roll the salmon slices around the shellfish. Cut each roll in half.

Beat the light vinaigrette and drizzle over the *mesclun* and tomato salad. Pour 3 tablespoons sauce in the centre of each plate and spread evenly with the back of a spoon. Arrange the salmon rolls on top of the sauce.

Garnish elegantly with the salmon or trout caviar and several sprigs of dill. Serve at room temperature or warm slightly by placing the plates in a hot oven for a moment.

Note: this recipe can be prepared with crayfish or diced lobster meat.

LITTLE LOBSTERS WITH GARDEN HERBS

SERVES 4

4 very small live lobsters, 300-350 g/10-12 oz each

SAUCE
coral and tomalley (greenish substance) from the lobsters
200 ml/7 fl oz very low-fat natural yogurt
1 tablespoon tomato ketchup
1 teaspoon strong Dijon-style mustard
1 tablespoon red wine vinegar
1 teaspoon Worcestershire sauce
¼ teaspoon Tabasco sauce
¼ teaspoon whisky

GARNISH
1 peach or mango
1 Granny Smith apple
1 tomato
4 black olives
2 tablespoons chopped chives
2 tablespoons tiny chervil sprigs
8 basil leaves, chopped
20 tarragon leaves

Preparation time: 35-40 minutes
Cooking time: 8 minutes

TO COOK THE LOBSTERS: bring a stockpot of unsalted water to the boil. Add the live lobsters, bring the water back to the boil, then cook for a further 8 minutes.

When the lobsters are cooked, remove them with a slotted spoon and place on a tea towel. Leave to cool for 20 minutes at room temperature.

TO PREPARE THE GARNISH AND THE LOBSTERS: peel the fruit and cut in tiny dice, about 3 mm/⅛ inch. Quarter the tomato and scoop out the inside of each quarter. Cut the tomato into the same size dice as the fruit. Stone the olives and chop finely. Set each ingredient aside separately in small bowls covered with cling film.

When the lobsters have cooled sufficiently, separate the heads from the tails and remove the coral and tomalley; set aside. Clean and set aside the heads.

TO PREPARE THE SAUCE: put the lobster coral and tomalley in a food processor with the remaining sauce ingredients. Process for 30 seconds to obtain a smooth consistency. Set aside at room temperature.

GARNISH AND PRESENTATION: shell the lobster tails and cut each tail into 1 cm/½ inch slices, keeping the shape of the tail intact. Remove the flesh from the lobster claws, also keeping the flesh intact and whole. Cover each plate with some sauce and arrange a lobster tail, cut up and re-formed, on top. Place a lobster head at the top of each plate to continue creating the body and place the shelled claws on either side of the body.

Combining the colours and flavours attractively, sprinkle each plate with the herbs, fruit and vegetables that were reserved for garnish. Serve immediately.

Note: you can prepare this dish in advance, keeping the plates in a cool place but not in the refrigerator.

Little Lobsters with Garden Herbs

PIZZA WITH SMOKED HAM AND SOYA BEAN SPROUTS

SERVES 4

PIZZA DOUGH
5 g/¼ oz fresh yeast
50 ml/2 fl oz warm water
50 g/2 oz strong plain flour
50 g/2 oz oat flakes
pinch of salt

PIZZA TOPPING
sprig of thyme
3 tablespoons chopped parsley
3 tablespoons chopped chives
100 g/4 oz 0% fat fromage frais
salt and pepper
3 thin slices of smoked ham or prosciutto
1 teaspoon olive oil
150 g/5 oz fresh soya bean sprouts
1 tablespoon safflower oil

Preparation time: 20 minutes
Cooking time: 12 minutes

TO PREPARE THE PIZZA DOUGH: dissolve the yeast in the warm water. Put the flour and oats in a food processor and process for 25-30 seconds. Add the yeast mixture and process until the dough is smooth and forms a ball. Transfer to a floured surface, form into a ball and allow to rest for 5-10 minutes.

Using your fingertips, lightly oil a nonstick baking sheet. Roll out the dough until very thin. Using a saucepan lid or flan tin 30 cm/12 inches in diameter as a guide, cut out a circle and place on the baking sheet.

TO PREPARE THE TOPPING: preheat the oven to 190°C/375°F/Gas Mark 5. Rub the sprig of thyme between your fingers to loosen the leaves. Mix all the herbs with the *fromage frais* and season with salt and pepper.

Trim the ham of any gristle or fat. Spread the olive oil over the pizza dough and cover with the slices of ham.

Spread the *fromage frais* mixture carefully over the ham. Toss the soya bean sprouts with the safflower oil and sprinkle over the pizza.

COOKING AND PRESENTATION: bake the pizza in the oven for 8 minutes. Lightly brown under the grill for 4 minutes, slide on to a platter and serve immediately.

'RICH' SCRAMBLED EGGS IN THEIR SHELLS

SERVES 4

8 very fresh eggs
1 matje herring (see note) or 75 g/3 oz smoked salmon
salt and pepper
1 tablespoon groundnut oil
2 tablespoons skimmed milk
1 heaped tablespoon chopped chives
50 g/2 oz caviar or salmon caviar

ACCOMPANIMENT
puffed rice cakes, cut into finger-size lengths with a serrated knife, or spring onions

Preparation time: 30-35 minutes
Cooking time: 5 minutes

TO PREPARE THE EGGS: with a very sharp knife, cleanly slice off the larger end of each egg. Without chipping the shells, empty the eggs into a bowl. Wash the eggshells and dry them by placing them cut side down on a tea towel. Cut the *matje* herring or smoked salmon into small cubes and set aside.

TO COOK THE EGGS: beat the eggs with a small whisk. Season lightly with salt and pepper. Pour the groundnut oil into a saucepan and add the beaten eggs. Scramble the eggs very gently over a low heat for 3-5 minutes, stirring constantly with a whisk, until they are set but very creamy. Remove from the heat, add the skimmed milk and the chives and continue to stir for 1 minute.

GARNISH AND PRESENTATION: fill each shell with the creamy scrambled eggs. Place in eggcups. Using a small spoon, garnish the top of 4 eggs with a little mound of caviar. Garnish the remaining 4 eggs with the herring or smoked salmon. Place 2 eggs with different garnishes on each plate. Serve with the rice cake fingers or spring onions.

Note: *matje* are young herrings that are caught before they spawn. They are then filleted and lightly salted.

SOFT-BOILED EGGS WITH AUBERGINE CAVIAR

SERVES 4

4 eggs (size 1)

AUBERGINE CAVIAR
1 aubergine, about 350 g/12 oz
sprig of thyme
1 bay leaf
1 red pepper
1 tablespoon olive oil
1 clove of garlic, finely chopped
1 onion, finely chopped
100 g/4 oz white mushrooms, finely chopped
1 tablespoon chopped parsley
1 tablespoon chopped basil
4 stoned black olives, finely chopped
salt and pepper

GARNISH
sprigs of parsley

Preparation time: 25-30 minutes
Cooking time: aubergine caviar: 1 hour; eggs: 5 minutes

TO PREPARE AND COOK THE AUBERGINE CAVIAR: preheat the oven to 180°C/350°F/Gas Mark 4.

Wrap the aubergine, thyme and bay leaf in foil. Cook in the oven for 1 hour.

Soft-boiled Eggs with Aubergine Caviar

Meanwhile, hold the red pepper with a long-handled fork and pass it over a gas flame until its skin blackens and blisters. (You can also place it under the grill.) Peel the pepper, cut it in half, remove the inner ribs and seeds and chop finely.

Heat the olive oil in a nonstick frying pan over a medium heat. Add the garlic, onion and mushrooms and fry gently until all the liquid has evaporated. Add the chopped red pepper, mix together and cook for 3 minutes more, making sure that all the moisture has evaporated. Set aside.

When the aubergine has finished cooking, remove the foil. Cut the aubergine open lengthwise, remove the flesh and place in a bowl. Mash and chop the flesh with a knife and fork. Add the mushroom and pepper mixture, the herbs and chopped olives and season with salt and pepper. Combine well to obtain a smooth mixture.

TO COOK THE EGGS: place the eggs in boiling water and cook for about 4½ minutes. Remove with a slotted spoon and refresh for 30 seconds in iced water. Shell them very carefully without breaking the egg whites, as the yolks will be soft. Place on a tea towel.

GARNISH AND PRESENTATION: divide the aubergine caviar, tepid or cold depending on your taste, between 4 plates. Place a soft-boiled egg on top of each one. Garnish with parsley sprigs and serve.

fISH AND SHELLFISH

STEAMED MONKFISH WITH 'MATIGNON' SAUCE

SERVES 4

500 g/1 ¼ lb monkfish, trimmed and sinews removed

'MATIGNON' SAUCE
2 carrots
2 onions
1 large or 2 small leeks
2 large celery sticks
500 ml/17 fl oz fish fumet *(see page 32) or poultry stock*
(see page 31)
1 bouquet garni
200 ml/7 fl oz white wine
15 g/½ oz cornflour
2 tablespoons cold water
2 tablespoons skimmed milk powder
juice of ½ lemon
1 tablespoon chopped parsley
1 tablespoon chopped chives
10 tarragon leaves, chopped

GARNISH
4 tablespoons chopped dill

Preparation time: 20-25 minutes
Cooking time: monkfish: 3 minutes; sauce: 12 minutes

TO PREPARE AND COOK THE 'MATIGNON' SAUCE: wash and peel all the vegetables and cut them into small, regular dice of about 5 mm/¼ inch. Bring the fish *fumet* or chicken stock to the boil, add the vegetables and the bouquet garni and cook for 4-5 minutes; the vegetables should still be firm. Pass through a sieve over a saucepan; leave the vegetables in the colander and reserve the cooking liquid.

Add the white wine to the vegetable cooking liquid in the saucepan. Bring to the boil and reduce until only about 450 ml/¾ pint of liquid remains. Dissolve the cornflour in the cold water, add to the reduced liquid and, stirring continuously with a spoon, boil for about 2 minutes or until thickened. Transfer the liquid to a food processor, add the skimmed milk powder and process for 20-25 seconds. Transfer the cooked vegetables from the colander to the saucepan, add the sauce and the lemon juice. Warm the mixture slowly, over a very low heat, stirring gently from time to time.

TO PREPARE AND COOK THE MONKFISH: cut the monkfish into small slices about 5 mm/¼ inch thick. Steam in a metal or bamboo steamer for 3 minutes. Remove from the steamer and drain on a tea towel.

GARNISH AND PRESENTATION: add the chopped herbs to the hot 'Matignon' sauce. Arrange the cooked monkfish slices attractively on four individual warmed plates, pour the sauce round the monkfish and garnish with the chopped dill. Serve immediately.

MONKFISH ESCALOPES WITH SAFFRON SAUCE

SERVES 4

400 g/14 oz monkfish, central bone removed
salt and pepper
tiny sprigs of chervil and flat-leaf parsley
tarragon leaves
4 anchovy fillets preserved in coarse salt
2 pinches of powdered saffron
2 tablespoons olive oil

SAUCE

200 ml/7 fl oz mussel cooking liquid (see page 89)
2 tablespoons olive oil
12 coriander seeds, crushed
pinch of saffron threads
pinch of thyme flowers (or use thyme leaves if unavailable)
2 tablespoons chopped herbs (chervil, chives, tarragon and
flat-leaf parsley)

VEGETABLES

100 g/4 oz mousserons or field mushrooms (see note on
page 60)
1 tomato
1 courgette
rind of 1 lemon
2 tablespoons olive oil

GARNISH

sprigs of chervil

Preparation time: 30-35 minutes
Cooking time: about 8 minutes

TO PREPARE THE MONKFISH: slice the monkfish into 12 pieces about 1 cm/½ inch thick with a filleting knife. Slice almost through each piece as if making a pocket and season with salt and pepper. Stuff chervil and parsley sprigs and tarragon leaves into each incision. Then add a third of an anchovy fillet and close the incision. Sprinkle the monkfish with the powdered saffron and drizzle with the olive oil. Set aside in the refrigerator.

TO PREPARE AND COOK THE SAUCE: put the mussel cooking liquid, olive oil, crushed coriander seeds, saffron threads and thyme flowers into a small saucepan. Boil for 1 minute, correct the seasoning and keep warm.

TO PREPARE THE VEGETABLES: trim and clean the mushrooms. With a small knife, remove the stem of the tomato, dip in boiling water for 10 seconds and immediately refresh. Peel the tomato, quarter and seed, then cut into 5 mm/¼ inch dice and set aside in the refrigerator.

Trim the ends off the courgette, core and cut into 1 cm/½ inch dice. Set aside in the refrigerator. Finely julienne the lemon rind, place in a small saucepan of water and boil for 2 minutes. Refresh in cold water, drain and set aside.

Pour the olive oil into a nonstick frying pan. Fry the courgette and mushrooms gently until both are golden brown. Keep warm.

TO COOK THE MONKFISH AND FINISH THE SAUCE: heat a nonstick frying pan coated lightly with olive oil and fry the monkfish escalopes on both sides very quickly, until just coloured.

Add the courgette, mushrooms, tomato and julienned lemon zest to the sauce. Add the chopped herbs and mix well.

PRESENTATION: pour some of the vegetable and sauce mixture on to 4 fish plates and arrange the monkfish escalopes on top. Garnish with the chervil sprigs.

Note: if fresh anchovy fillets packed in coarse salt are not available you can replace them with a can of anchovies in brine.

*Mackerel Fillets Marinated in
White Wine and Coriander*

MACKEREL FILLETS MARINATED IN WHITE WINE AND CORIANDER

SERVES 4

4 large mackerel, filleted (ask your fishmonger to do this)

MARINADE
120 ml/4 fl oz water
2 carrots, finely sliced
300 ml/½ pint white wine
2 tablespoons coriander seeds
2 large onions, finely sliced
1 lemon, finely sliced
sprig of thyme
1 bay leaf
1 parsley stalk
100 ml/3½ fl oz white wine vinegar
20 peppercorns
½ tablespoon salt

GARNISH
sprigs of dill

Preparation time: 15 minutes, plus marinating overnight
Cooking time: 5 minutes

TO PREPARE THE FISH: remove any stray bones from the mackerel fillets with tweezers.

TO COOK THE MARINADE: Bring the water to the boil in a medium saucepan. Add the carrots and cook for 2 minutes. Add the remaining marinade ingredients. Bring to the boil and cook over a high heat for 1 minute.

PRESENTATION: lay the mackerel fillets in a fairly deep glass serving dish. Pour in the marinade, making sure it covers the fish. Cover with cling film and refrigerate at least overnight. Garnish with sprigs of dill before serving.

Note: to serve warm. Remove the cling film and place in a warm oven, 180°C/350°F/Gas Mark 4, for 1 minute.

TROUT QUENELLES COOKED IN TROUT SKIN

SERVES 4

4 fresh trout, about 250 g/9 oz each
1 tablespoon olive oil

MOUSSE
2 egg whites
2 pinches of salt
150 g/5 oz 0% fat fromage frais
pinch of nutmeg
pepper
2 tablespoons chopped parsley

PURÉE
1 teaspoon olive oil
1 onion, chopped
1 tablespoon chopped savory
275 g/10 oz frozen petits pois
2 tablespoons water
salt and pepper
150 ml/¼ pint poultry stock (see page 31)

GARNISH
1 lemon, cut into wedges
sprigs of fresh savory

Preparation time: 30-35 minutes, plus 30 minutes resting
Cooking time: quenelles: 6 minutes; purée: 7 minutes

Ask your fishmonger to fillet the trout by first removing the skin of each fish without tearing it, which he should give you together with the fillets.

TO PREPARE THE MOUSSE: if there are any bones left in the trout fillets, remove them and cut each fillet into 2-3 pieces.

Place them in the freezer for 5 minutes.

Place half the trout in a food processor and process for 20 seconds, add 1 egg white and a pinch of salt and process for 10 seconds. Add half the *fromage frais* and process for 10 seconds more. Transfer the mixture to a bowl and refrigerate.

Repeat the above step with the remaining half of the fish, salt and *fromage frais* and the remaining egg white, then add to the first batch of mousse. Add the nutmeg, pepper and chopped parsley and combine well. Refrigerate the mousse for 30 minutes.

TO PREPARE THE QUENELLES: lay the trout skins on a work surface, shiny side down. Place a spoonful of the chilled mousse on each skin and wrap into a round, tight little packet. Set aside.

TO PREPARE AND COOK THE PURÉE: heat the olive oil over a medium heat in a small saucepan. Add the onion and savory, cover and cook gently for 2 minutes. Add the *petits pois*, water and salt, cover and cook for 5 more minutes.

Remove about half the peas with a slotted spoon and keep them warm in a separate saucepan with a tablespoon of the chicken stock. Place the rest in a food processor, add the remaining stock and process for 30 seconds, until smooth. Return to the saucepan, correct the seasoning with salt and pepper and keep warm in a double boiler.

TO COOK THE QUENELLES: heat the tablespoon of olive oil in a large nonstick frying pan. When the oil is very hot, add the trout quenelles and fry for 3 minutes on each side. Drain on kitchen paper.

GARNISH AND PRESENTATION: spread some hot purée on 4 warmed plates. Place 2 quenelles on top, sprinkle with the reserved petits pois, drained, garnish with a lemon wedge and a sprig of savory and serve immediately.

VEGETABLE AND SOLE BUNDLES 'RÉGENCE'

SERVES 2

50 g/2 oz carrots
25 g/1 oz celeriac
25 g/1 oz courgette
25 g/1 oz French beans
6 small sole fillets (200 g/7 oz total)
salt and pepper
300 g/11 oz spinach
6 crayfish

SAUCE
1 shallot, coarsely chopped
2 white mushrooms, very finely chopped
50 ml/2 fl oz white wine
200 ml/7 fl oz mussel cooking liquid (see page 89)
sprig of tarragon
10 g/¼ oz cooked, shelled mussels
1 tablespoon 0% fat fromage frais
1 tablespoon chopped herbs

GARNISH
sprigs of chervil
sprigs of thyme
sprigs of rosemary

Preparation time: 35-40 minutes
Cooking time: 20-25 minutes

TO PREPARE THE BUNDLES: trim the carrots, celeriac, courgette and French beans into small sticks 3 mm/⅛ inch thick and 6 cm/2½ inch long.

Cook each trimmed vegetable separately in a small saucepan of salted boiling water for 1-2 minutes, refresh in iced water and drain on a tea towel.

Make 6 bundles of mixed vegetable sticks and wrap each bundle in a sole fillet. Season with salt and pepper.

TO PREPARE THE SPINACH: wash and remove the stems from the spinach leaves and cook in salted boiling water. Refresh immediately, drain and press down to remove excess moisture. Set aside in the refrigerator.

TO COOK THE BUNDLES: preheat the oven to 190°C/375°F/Gas Mark 5.

Spread the chopped shallot and mushrooms for the sauce in an ovenproof dish. Pour in the white wine and mussel cooking liquid.

Arrange the fish and vegetable bundles and the crayfish in the dish. Add the sprig of tarragon. Cover the dish with a sheet of foil and bake in the oven for 10 minutes.

Take the dish out of the oven and remove the fish bundles and crayfish with a slotted spoon. Peel the crayfish tails, leaving the heads on. Set aside and keep warm.

TO PREPARE THE SAUCE: pour the cooking juice from the vegetable and sole bundles together with the shallot, mushrooms and tarragon into a food processor. Add the cooked mussels and the *fromage frais*. Process until puréed and pass through a fine-mesh sieve into a saucepan. Add the chopped herbs, correct the seasoning and keep the sauce warm in a double boiler.

GARNISH AND PRESENTATION: heat a nonstick frying pan and place the spinach in it. Season with salt and pepper, cover and heat through. Pour some sauce on each plate and arrange 3 bundles on each one with a crayfish and a small mound of spinach in between each bundle. Garnish with the chervil, thyme and rosemary sprigs.

SEA BREAM WITH VEGETABLES
À LA NIÇOISE

SERVES 4

4 sea bream fillets, 120 g/4 ½ oz each
aubergine caviar (see page 81)
150 ml/ ¼ pint fish fumet (see page 32)
salt and pepper

SAUCE
4 very ripe tomatoes
1 tablespoon tomato purée
2 tablespoons olive oil
1 teaspoon pastis (Ricard)
salt and pepper
1 tablespoon chopped dill

GARNISH
sprigs of herbs

Preparation time: 35-40 minutes
Cooking time: 5 minutes

TO PREPARE THE SEA BREAM: preheat the oven to 220°C/
425°F/Gas Mark 7.

Lightly oil a baking sheet and arrange the 4 sea bream
fillets on it. Cover the sea bream with the cold aubergine
caviar and set aside.

TO PREPARE THE SAUCE: dip the tomatoes into boiling water
for 30 seconds, peel, halve and seed. Cut into pieces and
place in a food processor. Add the tomato purée, olive oil,
pastis, salt and pepper and process at high speed to obtain a
smooth purée. Pass the mixture through a sieve into a small
saucepan and warm over a low heat.

TO COOK THE SEA BREAM: place the fish in the oven and cook
for 5 minutes. Remove the baking sheet and place the fish on
4 heated plates. Keep warm.

Sea Bream with Vegetables à la Niçoise

Pour the fish *fumet* into the baking sheet and, with a wooden spoon, deglaze and scrape the bits clinging to the surface, stirring the liquid well. Pour through a sieve into a pan, bring to the boil and season with salt and pepper.

GARNISH AND PRESENTATION: pour some of the *fumet* over each fillet. Stir the chopped dill into the lukewarm tomato sauce and pour into a warmed sauceboat. Serve the sea bream with the tomato sauce on the side. Garnish with a selection of herbs.

Note: you can replace the sea bream with chicken breasts. The fish *fumet* should then be replaced by chicken stock.

STEAMED SEA BASS WITH VEGETABLES MARINIÈRES

SERVES 4

4 pieces of sea bass, 100 g/4 oz each
500 ml/17 fl oz mussel cooking liquid (see note right)
50 ml/2 fl oz white wine
1 bouquet garni
6 basil leaves, chopped
1 clove of garlic, chopped
salt and pepper
tiny sprigs of parsley
tiny sprigs of chervil

VEGETABLES

4 miniature carrots with tops
4 miniature turnips with tops
4 miniature leeks
8 cloves of garlic, unpeeled
4 baby spring onions with stems
pinch of Nutrasweet sweetener

Preparation time: 15-20 minutes
Cooking time: about 30 minutes

TO PREPARE AND COOK THE VEGETABLES: scrape the carrots and turnips. Trim off all but 4-5 cm/1½-2 inches of the leaves. Trim the leeks, keeping only the white and the tenderest part of the green. Wash well. Remove only the outermost layer of skin from the garlic cloves and spring onions.

Cook the miniature carrots and turnips in salted boiling water for 8-10 minutes with the pinch of sweetener. The vegetables should remain firm. Cook the leeks in salted boiling water for about 3 minutes. Cook the garlic cloves and spring onions in salted boiling water for 5-6 minutes. Drain and refresh each vegetable.

TO COOK THE SEA BASS: arrange the cooked vegetables in a cast-iron stockpot and carefully pour in the mussel cooking liquid and the white wine. Bring to the boil. Place the sea bass and the bouquet garni in the pot, cover and simmer gently for 7 minutes. Remove from the heat and steam, covered, for 2 minutes.

PRESENTATION: with a slotted spoon, remove the sea bass and vegetables; discard the bouquet garni. Arrange the turnips and carrots in the shape of a fan on one side of each warmed plate.

Arrange the other vegetables on the opposite side of each plate and place a piece of sea bass in the centre. Keep the plates warm until you finish preparing the sauce.

TO FINISH THE SAUCE: place the stockpot over a high heat and add the chopped basil and garlic. Bring to the boil and reduce the sauce to a quarter of its original volume. Correct the seasoning with salt and pepper, pass through a fine-mesh sieve and add the sprigs of parsley. With a spoon, pour some sauce over the sea bass and vegetables on each plate. Sprinkle with chervil sprigs.

Note: the mussel cooking liquid is obtained from preparing a dish of *moules marinières*. Filter the liquid before using in this recipe. The shelled mussels make an excellent hors-d'oeuvre served with mayonnaise.

ROLLED SKATE WITH CHICORY

SERVES 4

4 skate wings, 250 g/9 oz each
175 ml/6 fl oz water
1 tablespoon white wine vinegar
salt

SAUCE AND CHICORY
750 g/1 ¾ lb chicory heads
1 teaspoon olive oil
1 shallot, finely chopped
pinch of nutmeg
100 ml/3 ½ fl oz fish fumet *(see page 32)*
juice of 3 limes
1 teaspoon cornflour
1 tablespoon water
salt and pepper

GARNISH
1 tomato
40 nicely shaped chicory leaves
1 tablespoon olive oil
pinch of sugar
salt and pepper
2 tablespoons chopped chives

Preparation time: 15 minutes
Cooking time: skate: 6 minutes; chicory: 4 and 10 minutes

TO PREPARE THE SKATE: rinse the skate wings under running water and drain on a tea towel.

TO PREPARE THE VEGETABLES AND SAUCE: wash the chicory heads and set aside 40 of the best leaves. Finely chop the remaining chicory into short strips.

Heat the olive oil in a small frying pan over a medium heat, add the shallot and soften for 1-2 minutes. Add the chopped chicory and the nutmeg and cook, stirring occasionally, for 3-4 minutes, until the chicory is soft and any liquid has evaporated. Remove from the heat and set aside.

Bring the fish *fumet* and lime juice to the boil in a saucepan. Add the cornflour, dissolved in the cold water, and boil for 2-3 minutes, stirring all the time. Pour into a food processor, add 2 tablespoons of the cooked chicory, and process for 30 seconds until smooth and creamy. Return the sauce to the pan. Season with salt and pepper and keep warm over a very low heat.

TO PREPARE THE GARNISH: dip the tomato into boiling water for 30 seconds, then peel. Quarter, seed and dice; set aside.

In a large bowl, combine the whole chicory leaves with the olive oil, sugar, salt and pepper. Spread on a baking sheet, making sure they are not overlapping.

TO COOK THE SKATE AND CHICORY LEAVES: preheat the oven to 180°C/350°F/Gas Mark 4.

Put the water, vinegar and salt in a large frying pan. Bring to the boil. Add the skate wings, black skin face down, and simmer, covered, for 3 minutes on each side. Remove from the heat.

Meanwhile, place the whole chicory leaves in the oven for 10 minutes. For the last few minutes, brown them under the grill. Reheat the chopped chicory and set aside. Remove the skate from the frying pan with a fish slice, place on a tea towel and keep warm.

GARNISH AND PRESENTATION: place some chopped chicory and the skate on 4 very hot plates and arrange the browned chicory leaves next to them. Pour the heated sauce over the skate, sprinkle with the diced tomato and chopped chives. Serve immediately.

Rolled Skate with Chicory

OPEN RAVIOLI WITH SHRIMPS IN GINGER SAUCE

SERVES 4

PLAIN RAVIOLI

100 g/4 oz plain flour
50 g/2 oz egg white

GREEN RAVIOLI

20 g/¾ oz parsley
100 g/4 oz plain flour
40 g/1½ oz egg white

STUFFING

175 g/6 oz tiny peeled shrimps
100 g/4 oz carrots
100 g/4 oz leeks
100 g/4 oz celery
50 g/2 oz white mushrooms
1 teaspoon olive oil
2 tablespoons water
sprig of thyme
1 bay leaf
2 tablespoons chopped parsley
salt and pepper

SAUCE

15 g/¾ oz fresh root ginger
100 ml/3½ fl oz white wine
100 ml/3½ fl oz fish fumet or poultry stock (see pages 32 or 31)
1 teaspoon cornflour
1 tablespoon cold water

Preparation time: 40-45 minutes
Cooking time: stuffing: about 8 minutes; ravioli dough: 3-4 minutes

TO PREPARE THE RAVIOLI DOUGH: place the ingredients for the plain ravioli in a food processor. Process for 20 seconds to obtain a smooth dough. Form into a ball on the work surface.

Chop the parsley and place in the food processor with the remaining green ravioli ingredients. Process for 20 seconds to obtain a dough. Form into a ball on the work surface.

With a rolling pin, roll out each ball of dough into a thin sheet about 2 mm/¹⁄₁₀ inch thick, or use a pasta machine. Use a small pastry wheel or small, sharp knife to cut each sheet into 4 pieces about 10 cm/4 inches square. Dust lightly with flour and cover with a tea towel.

TO PREPARE AND COOK THE STUFFING: wash all the vegetables, peel where necessary, and cut each into regular 5 mm/¼ inch dice. Heat the olive oil in a frying pan over a low heat, add the vegetables, water, thyme and bay leaf and cook, covered, for 8 minutes, stirring occasionally. When the vegetables are just tender, add the shrimps (reserving 4 for garnish) and parsley, season with salt and pepper and keep warm on the side of the cooker.

Open Ravioli with Shrimps in Ginger Sauce

TO PREPARE AND COOK THE SAUCE: peel the ginger, cut into pieces and place in a food processor with the white wine and fish *fumet* or poultry stock. Process for 30 seconds and pass through a fine-mesh sieve into a saucepan.

Bring this liquid to the boil for 2 minutes, add the cornflour, dissolved in the cold water, and, beating constantly with a small whisk, boil for 2 more minutes. Reduce the heat to very low and keep warm.

TO COOK THE RAVIOLI DOUGH: add the squares of dough one by one to a large saucepan of salted boiling water, cook for 3-4 minutes and place on a tea towel to drain.

GARNISH AND PRESENTATION: on 4 warmed plates, place a square of green dough and cover with the vegetable and shrimp mixture. Place on top a square of white dough, then pour the ginger sauce over. Garnish each plate with a reserved shrimp. If the ravioli pieces cool while you are arranging them, place the plates, 2 at a time, in a hot oven for 1-2 minutes before serving.

Note: if you substitute shop-bought green and plain lasagne for the homemade ravioli dough, cook the lasagne first before cutting it into squares.

BAKED NEW POTATOES TOPPED WITH SMOKED SALMON AND ANCHOVIES

SERVES 4

12 small new potatoes, about 75 g/3 oz each
1 slice of smoked salmon (about 75 g/3 oz)
8 small anchovy fillets in brine
200 g/7 oz 0% fat fromage frais
25 g/1 oz chopped herbs: chives, parsley and tarragon
juice of ½ lemon
pepper
1 small shallot

Preparation time: 30-35 minutes
Cooking time: 30-40 minutes

Baked New Potatoes Topped with
Smoked Salmon and Anchovies

TO COOK THE POTATOES: preheat the oven to 190°C/375°F/Gas Mark 5.

Wash the potatoes well, dry carefully and put on the middle shelf of the oven.

TO PREPARE THE TOPPINGS: combine the *fromage frais* with the chopped herbs, adding the lemon juice and pepper. Set aside.

Cut the smoked salmon into thin strips. Peel the shallot and slice very finely. Wipe the anchovies with a piece of kitchen paper and cut into 1 cm/½ inch pieces.

GARNISH AND PRESENTATION: when the potatoes are cooked, allow them to cool slightly, then make a lengthwise cut in each. Pinch the potatoes to open and and remove a small amount of potato. Garnish each potato with some of the *fromage frais* mixture. Top 4 potatoes with smoked salmon and shallot. Top 4 others with anchovies.

Serve 3 potatoes on each plate, one with just fromage frais, one with smoked salmon and one with anchovy.

Note: you can also wrap each potato in foil and bake for 30 minutes on a barbecue instead of in the oven.

SALMON WITH A TART SAUCE 'GEORGES BLANC'

SERVES 4

500 g/1 ¼ lb salmon fillet, in one piece
4 drops of olive oil

SAUCE
100 g/4 oz 0% fat fromage frais
1 tablespoon red wine vinegar
1 tablespoon olive oil
2 tablespoons lukewarm water
1 teaspoon Worcestershire sauce
juice of ½ lemon
salt and pepper
1 tablespoon chopped parsley
1 tablespoon chopped chervil
10 tarragon leaves, chopped
2 basil leaves (optional)

GARNISH
sprigs of herbs

Preparation time: 20-25 minutes
Cooking time: 2 minutes

TO PREPARE THE SALMON: preheat the oven to 200°C/400°F/ Gas Mark 6.

Using your fingers, oil 4 ovenproof plates with the olive oil. Remove the skin from the salmon. With an extremely sharp knife, slice the salmon into very thin slices. Arrange them on the plates and set aside.

TO PREPARE THE SAUCE: place all the sauce ingredients except the herbs in a bowl. Beat the mixture with a whisk until it is thick enough to coat a spoon lightly. Correct the seasoning with salt and pepper. Set aside at room temperature.

COOKING AND PRESENTATION: place the plates, 2 at a time, in the oven for 1-1½ minutes. Quickly mix the chopped herbs into the sauce and pour some sauce on each plate, spreading it around the fish with the back of a spoon. Garnish with the sprigs of herbs and serve immediately.

GRILLED TUNA STEAKS WITH FRESH TOMATO SAUCE

SERVES 4

2 thick slices of fresh tuna, about 250 g/9 oz each
400 g/14 oz fresh tomato sauce (see page 38), kept hot
10 basil leaves, coarsely chopped

MARINADE
1 clove of garlic, peeled
sprig of thyme
1 tablespoon olive oil
salt and pepper

Preparation time: 15 minutes, 1-2 hours in advance
Cooking time: 5 minutes

TO PREPARE THE TUNA AND MARINADE: cut each slice of tuna in half to obtain 4 large steaks. Rub a glass dish with the peeled clove of garlic. Rub the sprig of thyme with your fingers over the dish so that the leaves are sprinkled over the surface. Drizzle with the olive oil and sprinkle with salt and pepper. Place the tuna steaks on the dish and turn them several times to coat with the oil mixture. Marinate for 1-2 hours, turning them regularly.

TO COOK THE TUNA: heat the grill and grill the tuna steaks for 2½ minutes on each side.

GARNISH AND PRESENTATION: add 2 tablespoons hot water and the chopped basil to the tomato sauce. Spoon some tomato sauce on to 4 plates or spoon it all on to a serving dish. Place the tuna steaks next to the sauce and serve.

Note: you can accompany this dish with Gratin of Courgettes and Onions (see page 127) or Braised Fennel (see page 123).

Grilled Tuna Steaks with Fresh Tomato Sauce

SAUTÉED SALMON FILLETS WITH CURRY SAUCE

SERVES 4

4 salmon fillets, 100 g/4 oz each
1 teaspoon olive oil
salt and pepper
1 tablespoon curry powder
4 tiny sprigs of flat-leaf parsley

SAUCE

1 teaspoon olive oil
250 g/9 oz mushrooms, trimmed, washed and quartered
2 shallots, chopped
1 tablespoon curry powder
150 ml/¼ pint white wine
100 ml/3½ fl oz fish fumet (see page 32)
1 tablespoon skimmed milk powder
1 tablespoon 0% fat fromage frais
salt and pepper
2 tablespoons chopped chives

Preparation time: 15 minutes
Cooking time: sauce: about 10 minutes; salmon: about 1 minute

TO PREPARE AND COOK THE SAUCE: heat the olive oil in a pan, over a high heat, add the mushrooms, shallots and curry powder. Cook quickly until any liquid has evaporated. Place in a food processor and process for about 20 seconds. Return to the pan and add the white wine and fish *fumet*. Bring to the boil and reduce for about 5 minutes until the purée is rather thin. Add the milk powder, *fromage frais* and salt and pepper. Mix well and keep warm.

TO PREPARE AND COOK THE SALMON: remove any bones and the skin from the salmon fillets.

Heat the olive oil in a large frying pan over a high heat. Season the salmon fillets on both sides with salt, pepper and the curry powder. Press a sprig of parsley on one side of each fillet. When the oil is very hot, add the fillets, parsley-side down. Cook for about 30 seconds on each side. The salmon should be neither underdone nor overdone. With a fish slice, remove the fillets and place on paper towels.

PRESENTATION: add the chopped chives to the sauce. If the sauce seems too thick, thin with a little hot water. Pour the sauce on to 4 plates and place the salmon fillets on top. Serve.

SCALDED TURBOT WITH FENNEL AND OLIVE OIL 'GUALTIERO MARCHESI'

SERVES 4

450 g/1 lb small turbot (or any white firm-fleshed fish)
2 large fennel bulbs
4 small sprigs of dill
4 tablespoons virgin olive oil
750 ml/1¼ pints water
1 teaspoon salt
pepper

Preparation time: 10 minutes
Cooking time: 5 minutes

TO PREPARE AND COOK THE FENNEL: bring the water to the boil with the salt added. Trim and wash the fennel bulbs; cut each lengthwise into thin slices, about 3 mm/⅛ inch thick. When the water is boiling, add the fennel and cook for 4-5 minutes. Remove the saucepan from the heat and set aside.

TO PREPARE THE FISH: heat the oven to 220°C/425°F/Gas Mark 7. Remove the skin and bones from the fish, cut into thin strips 5 mm/¼ inch thick and arrange on 4 shallow soup plates.

COOKING AND PRESENTATION: coarsely chop the dill sprigs. Bring the fennel back to the boil, add the olive oil, dill and 16 turns of the pepper mill. Place the plates of fish in the oven for 1 minute. Put the plates on the table and pour a ladleful of fennel and its cooking liquid into each.

MUSSEL AND VEGETABLE PAELLA

SERVES 4

1 kg/2 ¼ lb mussels
200 ml/7 fl oz white wine

VEGETABLES
200 g/7 oz fresh soya bean sprouts
2 onions
2 carrots
2 celery sticks
1 clove of garlic
1 tablespoon olive oil
120 g/4 ½ oz long-grain rice
400 ml/14 fl oz water
3 generous pinches of saffron
1 bouquet garni
salt and pepper

GARNISH
2 tablespoons chopped parsley

Preparation time: 30-35 minutes
Cooking time: 30 minutes; mussels: 3-4 minutes

TO PREPARE THE MUSSELS AND VEGETABLES: scrape the mussels and wash them in several changes of water. Set aside in a large container of water.

Wash the soya bean sprouts, dip them into boiling water for 1 minute, drain and set aside. Peel and wash the other vegetables and slice finely.

TO COOK THE RICE AND VEGETABLES: heat the oil over a medium heat in a large saucepan. Add the rice and fry gently for 1 minute. Add the sliced onions, carrots, celery and garlic, mix with the rice, and continue to fry gently for 2 more minutes, stirring constantly. Add the water, saffron, bouquet garni, salt and pepper. Quickly bring to the boil, mixing the ingredients with a spatula. Lower the heat, cover and simmer for 20 minutes.

TO COOK THE MUSSELS: put the white wine in a stockpot over a high heat. Drain the mussels, add them to the pot and cook for 4 minutes. Remove them with a slotted spoon, draining off all the liquid, discard any which do not open and leave the remainder to cool on a platter. Pass the mussel liquid into a bowl through a fine-mesh sieve lined with a double layer of muslin. Shell the mussels and set aside.

FINISHING AND PRESENTATION: 5 minutes before the rice and vegetables are cooked, add the mussel cooking liquid to the pan. When the rice is cooked, remove the bouquet garni, add the mussels and the soya bean sprouts to the pan, mix gently, cover and heat through for 5 minutes over a very low heat. Correct the seasoning with salt and pepper. Serve the paella in a serving dish, sprinkled with the chopped parsley.

Note: you can replace the mussels with prawns; peel the tails before adding to the rice and vegetables.

MEAT, POULTRY AND GAME

CHICKEN SAUSAGES WITH LEEKS

SERVES 4

4 skinned and boned chicken breasts, about 120 g/4¹⁄₂ oz each
4 thin slices of jambon de Bayonne *or prosciutto*

STUFFING
500 g/1 ¹⁄₄ lb leeks
2 tomatoes
salt and pepper

LEEK GARNISH
500 g/1 ¹⁄₄ lb leeks
1 tablespoon olive oil
salt and pepper

SAUCE
250 ml/8 fl oz white wine
2 shallots, very finely chopped
2 white mushrooms, very finely chopped
¹⁄₂ teaspoon curry powder
¹⁄₂ chicken stock cube
¹⁄₂ bay leaf
2 sprigs of tarragon
salt and pepper
2 teaspoons cornflour
1 tablespoon cold water
1 tablespoon 0% fat fromage frais
2 teaspoons tomato ketchup

Preparation time: 35-40 minutes
Cooking time: sausages: 12 minutes; sauce: 5 minutes

TO PREPARE THE STUFFING AND THE GARNISH: cut the stem end off all the leeks, peel off the tough outer leaves and wash well under running water. Cut each leek in half lengthwise and cut in very thin strips, about 1 cm/¹⁄₂ inch wide, crosswise. Wash again. Place the leeks in a saucepan of salted boiling water and boil for 3 minutes. Drain, refresh under cold water and set aside.

Dip the tomatoes into boiling water for 30 seconds. Peel, cut into 6 pieces and seed. Set aside.

TO PREPARE AND COOK THE SAUSAGES: place the chicken breasts between 2 sheets of cling film and flatten well with the flat side of a wide knife blade. Remove the fat from the *jambon de Bayonne* or *prosciutto*.

On a work surface, lay out 4 pieces of foil 25 cm/10 inches square. Place a slice of *jambon de Bayonne* or *prosciutto* on each square, and place a chicken breast on top of that.

Take half the chopped leeks and squeeze to remove any excess water. Spread them over the chicken breasts and place 3 tomato pieces on each 'sausage'. Season lightly with salt and pepper. Roll each sausage tightly in the foil and twist the ends to seal. Steam in a metal or bamboo steamer for 12 minutes.

TO PREPARE THE SAUCE: place all the sauce ingredients in a small saucepan except for the cornflour, cold water, *fromage frais* and ketchup. Bring to the boil and cook for 3 minutes. Add the cornflour dissolved in the cold water and boil for 1 more minute. Pass through a fine-mesh sieve into a food processor. Add the *fromage frais* and ketchup, process for 15 seconds and correct the seasoning with salt and pepper.

Pour the sauce into a saucepan. Keep warm over a low heat or in a double boiler.

GARNISH AND PRESENTATION: heat the olive oil in a saucepan over a low heat, add the remaining leeks, season with salt and pepper and heat thoroughly. When the sausages are cooked, remove the foil and slice each into 5 rounds.

Spread some sauce on 4 heated plates. Arrange the sliced chicken sausages and the leek garnish on each plate. Serve immediately.

Note: the chicken breasts may be replaced by veal, turkey, lean pork or fish fillets. The leeks may be replaced by spinach or watercress.

TURKEY BREASTS COATED WITH SPICES

SERVES 4

4 skinless turkey breasts, about 120 g/4½ oz each
8 dried juniper berries, crushed
10 tarragon leaves, chopped
sprig of dill, chopped
1 tablespoon curry powder
1 teaspoon paprika
2 pinches of salt
1 teaspoon olive oil

SAUCE

25 g/1 oz carrot
25 g/1 oz celery
25 g/1 oz leek
25 g/1 oz mushrooms
tip of 1 clove of garlic
3 tablespoons water
200 ml/7 fl oz poultry stock (see page 31)
½ tablespoon red wine vinegar
1 tablespoon curry powder
pinch of saffron
1 teaspoon peanut butter
salt and pepper

Preparation time: 15-20 minutes
Cooking time: 8 minutes

TO PREPARE THE TURKEY BREASTS: place the juniper berries, tarragon and dill in a bowl, add the curry powder, paprika and salt and mix well. Coat the turkey breasts in this mixture, pressing down on them so that the spices stick; set aside on a plate.

TO PREPARE THE SAUCE: chop the garlic, cut the carrot, celery, leek and mushrooms into 5 mm/¼ inch dice and set aside.

TO COOK THE TURKEY BREASTS: preheat the oven to 140°C/275°F/Gas Mark 1.

Heat the oil over a medium heat in a nonstick frying pan and add the turkey breasts. Fry gently for 2 minutes on each side until golden, then transfer to a dish. Keep the turkey breasts warm in the oven.

TO COOK THE SAUCE: using the same frying pan, cook the garlic and diced vegetables in the water over a medium heat for 3 minutes, stirring them and scraping the bottom of the pan with a wooden spoon.

Add the poultry stock, vinegar, curry powder and saffron, mix and boil for 1 minute. Transfer the vegetables to a small saucepan with a slotted spoon and keep warm.

Beat the peanut butter into the liquid in the frying pan, correct the seasoning with salt and pepper and pour over the vegetables.

GARNISH AND PRESENTATION: spread the sauce on 4 warmed plates. Quickly cut each turkey breast on the diagonal into several slices and place on top of the sauce. Serve.

Note: you can accompany this dish with Stir-fried Beansprouts with Soy Sauce (page 129). You can also replace the turkey with another type of poultry, veal or pork.

Turkey Breasts coated with Spices

STUFFED CHICKEN BREASTS WITH COURGETTES AND ALMOND SAUCE

SERVES 2

2 large boneless chicken breasts, skinned
2 long courgettes
100 ml/3½ fl oz poultry stock (see page 31)
salt and pepper

TOMATO STUFFING
2 large ripe tomatoes
salt and pepper
1 teaspoon olive oil
1 teaspoon chopped shallot
1 clove of garlic, unpeeled
1 small bouquet garni
4 basil leaves, chopped

ALMOND SAUCE
85 ml/3 fl oz skimmed milk
1 teaspoon ground almonds
cooking liquid from the chicken breasts

GARNISH
chopped chives

Preparation time: 30 minutes
Cooking time: stuffing: 35 minutes; chicken: about
10 minutes

TO PREPARE THE ALMOND SAUCE: bring the skimmed milk to the boil in a saucepan and remove from the heat. Stir in the ground almonds until dissolved. Set aside, covered.

TO PREPARE THE TOMATO STUFFING: dip the tomatoes into boiling water for 15 seconds, refresh, peel, halve and seed. Cut the tomato halves in small dice and season with salt and pepper.

Heat the olive oil in a saucepan over a low heat, add the chopped shallot and sweat very gently in the oil for 5 minutes. Add the diced tomatoes, garlic and bouquet garni and cook, partially covered, for 30 minutes or until the cooking liquid has evaporated. Remove the garlic and bouquet garni. Add the chopped basil, correct the seasoning and keep warm over a very low heat.

TO PREPARE THE COURGETTES: trim off the ends of the courgettes. With a vegetable peeler, cut very thin slices down the length of each one. Cut each strip in half lengthwise so you end up with very long thin strips. Dip the courgette strips in boiling water for 30 seconds, then dip immediately into iced water. Drain on a tea towel.

TO COOK AND STUFF THE CHICKEN BREASTS: preheat the oven to 190°C/375°F/Gas Mark 5.

Heat the poultry stock, pour it into a small oval ovenproof dish and add the chicken breasts. Season with salt and pepper, cover with foil and cook in the oven for about 10 minutes. When the chicken is cooked, transfer it to a chopping board and pour the cooking liquid into a saucepan; set aside.

With a knife, cut a pocket in the thickest part of each chicken breast. Stuff each with a tablespoonful of the tomato mixture. Lay half the courgette strips side by side on the board and place a chicken breast on top. Wrap the chicken breast tightly in the courgette and repeat the step for the other chicken breast. Put them back in the oval dish and keep warm.

TO FINISH THE SAUCE: pass the almond milk through a sieve into the saucepan of chicken stock and reduce over a medium heat until only 120 ml/4 fl oz liquid remains. Meanwhile, heat the chicken breasts in the oven for 5 minutes.

PRESENTATION AND GARNISH: arrange the heated chicken breasts on warmed plates and surround with the almond sauce. Garnish with a few chopped chives and serve.

POUSSINS STUFFED WITH JULIENNED VEGETABLES

SERVES 4

4 poussins, about 300 g/11 oz each
salt and pepper

JULIENNED VEGETABLE STUFFING
3 large carrots
3 leeks
3 celery sticks
1 tablespoon olive oil
sprig of thyme
salt and pepper

SAUCE
4 litres/7 pints water
1 chicken stock cube
2 shallots, chopped
50 g/2 oz mushrooms, finely sliced
100 ml/3 ½ fl oz white wine
1 bouquet garni
2 tablespoons cornflour
2 tablespoons cold water
2 tablespoons skimmed milk powder
salt and pepper

GARNISH
sprigs of chervil

Preparation time: 45 minutes
Cooking time: poussins: about 20 minutes; stuffing: 6 minutes

TO PREPARE AND COOK THE VEGETABLE STUFFING: wash and peel the carrots and leeks. Cut the leeks and celery into thin strips and finely julienne the carrots.

Heat the olive oil in a saucepan over a low heat. Add the vegetables, the thyme, rubbed between the fingers, and season with salt and pepper. Cook very gently, covered, for about 6 minutes, stirring occasionally. Set aside.

TO PREPARE AND COOK THE POUSSINS: split the back of each chicken with a large knife. Bone, leaving only the drumstick ends and the wing tip bones.

Spread the chickens, skin side down, on a work surface and season with salt and pepper. Spread some vegetable julienne over each chicken. Close them up so that they resemble whole chickens. Wrap each in foil, twisting the ends tightly. Bring a large saucepan of water to a simmer, add the chickens and cook for about 20 minutes, keeping the water at a simmer.

TO PREPARE THE SAUCE: place the water, stock cube, shallots, mushrooms, white wine and bouquet garni in a saucepan. Bring to the boil and reduce over a high heat for 5 minutes. Add the cornflour, dissolved in the cold water, and the skimmed milk powder. Boil for 2 more minutes, stirring. Correct the seasoning with salt and pepper. Pass this sauce through a fine-mesh sieve into another saucepan and keep warm.

GARNISH AND PRESENTATION: when the chickens are cooked remove the foil. Cut the chickens open, arrange on 4 individual warmed plates, pour the sauce around and garnish with sprigs of chervil. Serve the chickens immediately with a selection of seasonal vegetables.

Poussins Stuffed with Julienned Vegetables

STUFFED CABBAGE À L'ANCIENNE

SERVES 4

1 Savoy or curly-leaf cabbage
4 carrots
150 ml/¼ pint veal stock (see page 33)
150 ml/¼ pint water

STUFFING

1 teaspoon olive oil
4 onions, chopped
1 clove of garlic, chopped
150 g/5 oz jambon de Bayonne or prosciutto, thickly sliced
200 g/7 oz chicken breast
1 egg white
75 g/3 oz 0% fat fromage frais
bunch of parsley, chopped
pinch of nutmeg
pepper

SAUCE

12 dried juniper berries
cooking liquid from the stuffed cabbage
1 tablespoon gin
1 teaspoon cornflour
1 tablespoon cold water

Preparation time: 35-40 minutes
Cooking time: 30 minutes

To PREPARE THE VEGETABLES: remove and discard the outermost leaves of the cabbage, cut away the stem and separate all the remaining leaves.

Scrape and wash the carrots and cut into julienne on a diagonal.

Blanch the cabbage leaves for 4 minutes in a large saucepan of salted boiling water. Remove the leaves with a slotted spoon, refresh under cold water and spread out on a tea towel to drain.

In the same saucepan, blanch the julienned carrots for 1 minute in boiling water, refresh, drain and set aside.

To PREPARE THE STUFFING: heat the olive oil in a frying pan over a medium heat and gently fry the chopped onions and garlic for 4 minutes. Remove with a slotted spoon and set aside on a plate.

Remove the fat from the *jambon de Bayonne* or *prosciutto*, cut into 1 cm/½ inch dice and set aside. Cut the chicken breast into several pieces, place in a food processor and process for 20 seconds. Add the egg white, process for 5 seconds, then add the *fromage frais* and process for 20 seconds more. In a large bowl, combine and mix well the chicken mixture, chopped parsley, fried onions and garlic, *jambon de Bayonne* or *prosciutto*, nutmeg and pepper.

To PREPARE THE STUFFED CABBAGE: choose the 8 best cabbage leaves, spread them out on a work surface and dry well. Coarsely chop the remaining cabbage leaves. Arrange some julienned carrots on each whole cabbage leaf, cover with a little stuffing and top with some chopped cabbage. Repeat once more, starting with some julienned carrots and ending with a little chopped cabbage. Gather each leaf up around the stuffing, place on a small square of double-thickness muslin, gather up the 4 corners and twist, squeezing the stuffed leaf until it is a compact ball. Carefully remove the muslin.

To COOK THE STUFFED CABBAGE: preheat the oven to 190°C/375°F/Gas Mark 5. Oil a baking dish and place the stuffed cabbage leaves on it, close to one another. Pour in the veal stock and water and bake the cabbage packets for 20 minutes, basting frequently. If they begin to brown too soon, cover them with a sheet of foil.

To PREPARE THE SAUCE AND PRESENTATION: crush the juniper berries with the blade of a large knife. When the stuffed cabbage leaves are cooked, remove from the baking dish, arrange on 4 warmed serving plates and keep warm.

Pour the cooking liquid into a small saucepan, add the juniper berries and gin and bring to the boil. Add the cornflour, dissolved in the cold water, and boil for 2 minutes. Pour the sauce round the stuffed cabbage leaves and serve immediately. You can pass the sauce through a sieve beforehand to remove the crushed juniper berries.

Stuffed Cabbage à l'Ancienne

ROAST CHICKEN WITH GRAPEFRUIT AND PINK PEPPERCORN SAUCE

SERVES 4

1 roasting chicken, about 1.5 kg/3¼ lb
1 tablespoon olive oil
salt and pepper

GRAPEFRUIT AND PINK PEPPERCORN SAUCE
2 yellow grapefruit
2 pink grapefruit
1 carrot
1 onion
1 celery stick
sprig of thyme
½ bay leaf
1 parsley stalk
100 ml/3½ fl oz veal stock (see page 33)
2 teaspoons cornflour
1 tablespoon cold water
2 tablespoons pink peppercorns in vinegar

GARNISH
1 yellow grapefruit
1 pink grapefruit

Preparation time: 15-20 minutes
Cooking time: 1 hour

TO PREPARE AND COOK THE CHICKEN: preheat the oven to 190°C/375°F/Gas Mark 5.

Rub the chicken with the olive oil and season with salt and pepper inside and out. Roast for 1 hour in a roasting tin, basting frequently.

TO PREPARE THE GARNISH: grate a little rind from the grapefruit skin and set aside. Peel both the grapefruit, removing the membrane as well as the skin. With a small knife, cut through on each side of the membranes dividing the segments and remove the segments. Set them aside.

TO PREPARE THE SAUCE: squeeze the juice from the 4 grapefruit and set aside. Peel and wash the carrot and onion and slice into thin rounds, together with the celery. Place these vegetables and the herbs around the chicken after it has been roasting for about 35-40 minutes. About 5 minutes before the chicken is cooked, pour the veal stock and reserved grapefruit juice around the vegetables, which should have begun to brown. With a spatula, mix the vegetables, scraping the bottom of the tin in order to flavour the cooking juices. Remove the chicken from the tin, drain and place on a dish. Keep warm.

Pass the chicken cooking juices through a fine-mesh sieve into a saucepan. You should have about 350 ml/12 fl oz liquid. If there is more, reduce over a high heat; if less, add a little more brown stock and grapefruit juice. Let the sauce rest for 5 minutes, then use a spoon to remove any fat from the surface. Bring to the boil and add the cornflour, dissolved in the cold water, and the drained pink peppercorns. Boil the sauce for 2 more minutes, stirring constantly. Lower the heat, keeping it warm, and heat the reserved grapefruit segments in the sauce.

GARNISH AND PRESENTATION: either carve the chicken into serving-size pieces or leave whole. Transfer to a warm serving platter, pour a little of the sauce round and garnish with the grapefruit segments and the reserved grapefruit rind. Serve the remaining sauce in a sauceboat.

Roast Chicken with Grapefruit and Pink Peppercorn Sauce

CALF'S LIVER WITH BEANS AND VEGETABLES

SERVES 4

1 thick slice of calf's liver, 150 g/5 oz
1 teaspoon olive oil
salt and pepper

BEANS AND VEGETABLES
25 g/1 oz dried black beans
25 g/1 oz dried haricot beans
25 g/1 oz green lentils de Puy
1 tomato
1 onion, chopped
1/4 clove of garlic, chopped
4 tablespoons red wine vinegar
100 ml/3 1/2 fl oz veal stock (see page 33)
100 g/4 oz petits pois, fresh or frozen
100 g/4 oz canned sweetcorn, drained
salt and pepper

GARNISH
2 tablespoons chopped chives

Preparation time: 20 minutes, plus soaking overnight
Cooking time: liver: 6 minutes; beans: at least 30 minutes

Calf's Liver with Beans and Vegetables

In separate bowls soak the dried black beans, haricot beans and lentils in water overnight and refrigerate.

TO COOK THE DRIED BEANS: Discard the soaking water and boil the dried beans and lentils separately in unsalted water for 10 minutes to destroy any harmful toxins. Discard the water again and then cook the dried beans and lentils separately in unsalted water for about 30 minutes or until tender, depending on the bean. Set aside in their cooking liquid.

TO COOK THE LIVER: preheat the oven to 140°C/275°F/Gas Mark 1. Heat the oil in a nonstick pan. When it is hot, add the liver, seasoned with salt and pepper, and cook for 3 minutes on each side. Remove from the pan with a fish slice, place on a plate and keep warm in the oven.

TO FINISH THE BEANS AND VEGETABLES: peel, seed and dice the tomato. Set aside. In the same pan used to cook the liver, fry the onion and garlic over a high heat for 1 minute, add the vinegar and veal stock, stirring and scraping the bottom of the pan. Boil down for 1 minute. Drain the cooked beans and lentils and add to the pan together with the *petits pois* and drained sweetcorn. Season with salt and pepper. Reheat, stirring, for 2 minutes. Add the diced tomato at the last minute.

PRESENTATION: arrange the beans and vegetables on 4 plates. Cut the liver into 5 mm/1/4 inch slices. Arrange in a fan shape on the vegetables, sprinkle with chives and serve.

HACHIS PARMENTIER OF SWEETBREADS AND TRUFFLES

SERVES 4

225 g/8 oz fresh calf's sweetbreads
25 ml/1 fl oz truffle juice (available in cans)
10 g/¼ oz truffle, chopped
150 g/5 oz carrots, peeled to the same diameter
25 g/1 oz truffle shavings

INGREDIENTS FOR BRAISING
20 g/¾ oz carrot
20 g/¾ oz leek
15 g/½ oz celery
15 g/½ oz onion
40 g/1½ oz white mushroom stalks
1 tablespoon groundnut oil
2 duck necks (substitute chicken or turkey necks if
unavailable)
salt and pepper, plus a few cracked peppercorns and a little
coarse salt
1 bouquet garni (thyme, bay leaf, parsley stalks and the
green part of leek)
50 ml/2 fl oz port
25 ml/1 fl oz Cognac
250 ml/8 fl oz veal stock (see page 33)

PURÉE
250 g/9 oz apples
200 g/7 oz celeriac
500 ml/17 fl oz water
50 g/2 oz skimmed milk powder
salt and pepper

GARNISH
4 sprigs of thyme or rosemary

Preparation time: about 40 minutes, plus 15 minutes the
night before
Cooking time: 40 minutes, plus 14 minutes just before
serving

TO PREPARE THE SWEETBREADS THE NIGHT BEFORE: place the sweetbreads in a bowl in the sink and let a continuous thin stream of cool water bathe them for 3-4 hours. Drain the sweetbreads on a tea towel, place them in a saucepan, cover with cold water and boil over a high heat for 3 minutes to blanch. Refresh them under cold running water, and, with a small knife, remove any connective tissue and tough membrane. Wrap them in a tea towel, place on a plate, cover with a rack and place some weights on top (these may be canned goods or any heavy object). Refrigerate overnight.

TO BRAISE THE SWEETBREADS: the next day, preheat the oven to 190°C/375°F/Gas Mark 5.

Peel, wash and cut into 5 mm/¼ inch dice all the vegetables listed for braising. Heat the groundnut oil in a stockpot, add the sweetbreads and the duck necks. Season with salt and pepper and brown lightly on all sides. Add the diced vegetables and bouquet garni and fry gently for 4-5 minutes.

Deglaze with the port and Cognac, scraping the bottom of the stockpot, then turn up the heat for 1 minute to evaporate the alcohol. Add the veal stock, season lightly with a few cracked peppercorns and a little coarse salt. Cover and cook in the oven for about 30 minutes. Remove the sweetbreads and duck necks from the stockpot and set aside in a bowl.

Transfer the vegetables and cooking liquid from the stockpot to a food processor. Purée and pass through a fine-mesh sieve into a bowl. Set aside.

TO PREPARE THE PURÉE: peel and core the apples, finely chop, and cook, covered, in a small saucepan with a few drops of water until they are very soft. Purée in a food processor. Peel the celeriac, cut into pieces, and cook until soft in the water mixed with the milk powder and a little salt. Drain and purée in a food processor. Combine the apple and celeriac purées and season with salt and pepper.

TO FINISH THE SWEETBREADS: separate the sweetbreads into smaller sections, taking care to remove any remaining connective tissue. Pick off the meat from the duck necks and pour the strained cooking liquid over both the sweetbreads and shredded duck meat. Add the truffle juice and chopped truffle, mix well and correct the seasoning.

To make the hachis parmentier: cut each carrot crosswise into rounds 3 mm/$\frac{1}{8}$ inch thick. Cook in salted boiling water for 2-3 minutes, then drain on a cloth.

Divide the sweetbread mixture between 4 small porcelain ramekins (7.5 cm/3 inch diameter and 4 cm/1$\frac{1}{2}$ inches high). Arrange some truffle shavings on top and finish with the apple and celeriac purée, filling the ramekins to 3 mm/$\frac{1}{8}$ inch from the top. Cover the purée with the carrot rounds, overlapping them a little. Cover each ramekin with cling film.

To cook the hachis parmentier: 20 minutes before serving, arrange the ramekins in a small roasting tin containing a little water. Cover the tin with foil and heat on the hob for 14 minutes, making sure the water barely simmers. Remove the cling film, garnish with thyme or rosemary and serve.

SPATCHCOCKED QUAILS WITH WILD MUSHROOMS

SERVES 4

8 quails, boned and flattened (ask your butcher to do this)
1 tablespoon olive oil
salt and pepper

MUSHROOMS
10 g/$\frac{1}{4}$ oz dried ceps
10 g/$\frac{1}{4}$ oz dried morels
200 g/7 oz fresh wild mushrooms (for example, mousserons,
chanterelles or trompettes de la mort, depending on the
season and availability)
200 ml/7 fl oz cold water
1 teaspoon olive oil
4 shallots, chopped
1 clove of garlic, chopped
100 ml/3$\frac{1}{2}$ fl oz white wine
50 ml/2 fl oz port
100 ml/3$\frac{1}{2}$ fl oz veal stock (see page 33)
2 teaspoons cornflour
1 tablespoon cold water
salt and pepper

GARNISH
chopped chives (optional)

Preparation time: 20-25 minutes
Cooking time: quails: 5-7 minutes; mushrooms: 8 minutes

To prepare the mushrooms: soak the dried ceps and morels in the cold water for 5-10 minutes. Trim the stem of the fresh mushrooms. Wash the mushrooms under a thin stream of water to remove traces of earth or sand, drain and dry carefully with a tea towel.

To cook the mushrooms: drain the dried mushrooms, reserving the liquid. Pass the liquid through several layers of muslin and set aside in a bowl.

Heat the olive oil in a large, nonstick frying pan over a high heat. Add all the mushrooms and fry for 5 minutes, stirring. Add the shallots and garlic, mix and fry for 1 more minute.

Still over a high heat, add the white wine and port, and deglaze by stirring the mushrooms and scraping the bottom of the pan with a wooden spoon for about 30 seconds. Add the veal stock and the reserved mushroom soaking liquid. Bring to a gentle boil and reduce by half. Add the cornflour, dissolved in the tablespoon of cold water and, stirring constantly, boil for 1 minute more. Transfer to a saucepan, season with salt and pepper and keep warm.

To cook the quails: preheat the grill. Arrange the quails, breast side up, on a baking sheet. Rub with the olive oil and season with salt and pepper. Grill for 5-7 minutes.

Garnish and presentation: place 2 quails on each plate. Pour the hot mushroom mixture over. If desired, sprinkle each portion with a few chopped chives. Serve immediately.

INDIVIDUAL RABBIT CHARLOTTES WITH HERB SAUCE

SERVES 4

1 rabbit, about 1.25 k g/2 ½ lb

MOUSSE
150 g/5 oz rabbit meat, cut from the saddle of above rabbit
pinch of salt
2 egg whites
50 g/2 oz 0% fat fromage frais
1 teaspoon thyme leaves

CHARLOTTES
the remaining rabbit
1 tablespoon olive oil
6 onions, coarsely sliced
2 cloves of garlic, coarsely sliced
2 celery sticks, coarsely sliced
300 ml/ ½ pint white wine
1 litre/1 ¾ pints poultry stock (see page 31) or water
1 bouquet garni
salt and pepper
2 small courgettes
3 tablespoons chopped herbs (chervil, parsley, chives, tarragon and basil)

SAUCE
cooking liquid from the rabbit
1 tablespoon cornflour
1 tablespoon cold water
salt and pepper
3 tablespoons chopped fresh herbs (as above)

VEGETABLE GARNISH
8 miniature carrots
8 miniature turnips
8 baby spring onions

Preparation time: 1 hour
Cooking time: rabbit: 2 hours; charlottes: 10 minutes

TO PREPARE AND COOK THE RABBIT: cut 150 g/5 oz meat from the saddle of the rabbit for the mousse and set aside. Cut the rest of the rabbit into 8 pieces.

Heat the olive oil in a frying pan over a high heat, add the rabbit pieces and fry until golden for about 5 minutes. Remove the rabbit with a slotted spoon and place the pieces in a casserole. In the same pan, fry the onions, garlic and celery for 5 minutes over a high heat. Add to the casserole containing the rabbit. Pour the white wine and poultry stock or water into the casserole and add the bouquet garni. Season with salt and pepper, cover, lower the heat and simmer gently for 2 hours.

TO PREPARE THE MOUSSE: cut the reserved rabbit meat into several pieces, place in a food processor and process for 15 seconds. Add a pinch of salt and the egg whites, process for 15 seconds, then add the *fromage frais* and thyme leaves and process for 15 seconds more. Transfer the mousse to a bowl and refrigerate.

TO PREPARE THE VEGETABLE GARNISH: wash and scrape the vegetables for the garnish, leaving about 4 cm/1 ½ inches of leafy top. Blanch them for 4 minutes in salted boiling water, refresh in cold water and set aside in a large saucepan with 175 ml/6 fl oz of their cooking liquid.

TO PREPARE AND COOK THE CHARLOTTES: when the rabbit pieces are cooked, transfer them with a slotted spoon to a plate and leave to cool. Transfer the vegetables from the casserole to a bowl with a slotted spoon and set aside.

Pass the rabbit cooking juices through a fine-mesh sieve into a saucepan and set aside.

Cut the unpeeled courgettes into thin rounds, blanch for 20 seconds in boiling water, drain and refresh in cold water. Drain again on a tea towel.

Cut all the rabbit meat from the bones with a small knife, cut the meat into slivers and set aside.

Oil 4 small glass or ceramic ramekin dishes and line each with a piece of cling film, making sure it extends a good way over the sides of the dish. Line the base with concentric circles of courgette slices and spread 5 mm/ ¼ inch of mousse over the sides of the dishes. Mix together the rabbit meat

*Individual Rabbit Charlottes
with Herb Sauce*

with the cooked vegetables from the casserole and the chopped herbs for the charlottes. Correct the seasoning with salt and pepper, fill each soufflé dish with this mixture and fold the cling film over the top of each charlotte.

Steam the charlottes for 10 minutes, either in a bamboo or metal steamer or in a covered saucepan containing enough water to come half-way up the sides of the dishes.

TO PREPARE AND COOK THE SAUCE: reduce the rabbit cooking liquid over a high heat, uncovered, to obtain 250 ml/8 fl oz. Dissolve the cornflour in the cold water, add to the cooking liquid, and, stirring constantly, boil for 2 more minutes. Correct the seasoning with salt and pepper and keep warm over a very low heat.

GARNISH AND PRESENTATION: reheat the reserved vegetable garnish. Unmould the charlottes on to kitchen paper and remove the cling film. Arrange the charlottes on 4 warmed plates. Mix the chopped herbs into the sauce and pour round the charlottes. Garnish with the heated, drained miniature vegetables and serve.

BONED ROAST VEAL WITH TOMATO AND BASIL SAUCE

SERVES 4

*1 loin of veal, about 1 kg/2 ¼ lb, boned and trimmed of all fat
1 teaspoon vegetable oil
salt and pepper
2 bay leaves
sprig of thyme
2 cloves of garlic*

SAUCE
*6 very ripe tomatoes
8 large basil leaves
large sprig of thyme
2 tablespoons olive oil
salt and pepper*

*Preparation time: 15 minutes
Cooking time: 25 minutes*

TO PREPARE AND COOK THE VEAL: preheat the oven to 190°C/375°F/Gas Mark 5. Rub the meat with the oil and season all over with salt and pepper. Heat a nonstick frying pan until very hot and lightly brown the meat on all sides. Place the meat in a roasting tin with the bay leaves, thyme and garlic and roast in the oven for 25 minutes, turning it over once half-way through cooking. Remove from the oven and allow it to rest for 5-10 minutes in a warm place.

TO PREPARE THE SAUCE: dip the tomatoes into boiling water for 30 seconds, peel, quarter, seed and cut into small dice. Drain the diced tomato in a small sieve. Coarsely chop the basil leaves. Rub the thyme between your fingers to release the leaves. Put the diced tomatoes in a saucepan. Add the olive oil, basil, thyme, salt and pepper, and heat very gently over a low heat without cooking the mixture.

GARNISH AND PRESENTATION: heat the veal in the hot oven for 3-4 minutes, then cut into 4 thick slices. Place a slice on each heated plate and surround with the warm sauce. Serve.

BEEF SIMMERED IN RED WINE

SERVES 4

500 g/1¼ lb lean stewing beef, cut into 4 cm/1½ inch cubes
(ask your butcher to do this)
1 large carrot
1 onion
1 clove of garlic
1 celery stick
2 tablespoons olive oil
1 bouquet garni
1 clove
sprig of tarragon
1 chicken stock cube
1 litre/1¾ pints red wine
250 ml/8 fl oz water
salt and pepper
25 g/1 oz sugar-free apple and pear spread (available from
health-food shops)
1 tablespoon cornflour
1 tablespoon cold water

VEGETABLE GARNISH
100 g/4 oz frozen petits pois
20 very small white mushrooms
100 ml/3½ fl oz water
pinch of salt
dash of lemon juice
20 baby spring onions
1 bunch of miniature carrots
20 miniature turnips or 20 radishes

Preparation time: 25-30 minutes
Cooking time: 2 hours

TO PREPARE AND COOK THE BEEF STEW: peel the carrot, onion and garlic and cut them into strips, together with the celery. Heat 1 tablespoon of the olive oil in a nonstick frying pan over a high heat and brown the beef on all sides. Transfer the meat with a slotted spoon to a casserole.

In the same pan, heat the remaining olive oil, add the vegetable strips and fry over a high heat for 4 minutes. Add the vegetables to the casserole.

Add the bouquet garni, clove, tarragon and stock cube to the beef and vegetables. Pour in the red wine and the water and bring to the boil. Season lightly with salt.

After a minute or so, lower the heat, cover and simmer gently for 1¾ hours.

TO PREPARE AND COOK THE VEGETABLE GARNISH: remove the *petits pois* from the freezer. Trim the mushrooms, wash, and place in a saucepan with the water, salt and lemon juice. Boil rapidly for 3-4 minutes. Remove from the heat and set aside.

Scrape and wash the miniature vegetables, leaving about 2.5 cm/1 inch of leafy top. Cook them in salted boiling water, counting 5 minutes from the moment the water returns to the boil. Drain, refresh in cold water and set aside.

TO FINISH THE STEW: when the meat is cooked, transfer the cubes with a slotted spoon to a plate. Pass the meat cooking juices through a fine-mesh sieve into a bowl, then pour back into the casserole. Reduce over a high heat until only about

Beef Simmered in Red Wine

250 ml/8 fl oz remains. Add the apple and pear spread and mix in. Pour in the cornflour, dissolved in the cold water. Boil the sauce for 2 minutes, stirring constantly, and correct the seasoning with salt and pepper. Add the beef to the sauce and heat for 5 minutes over a medium heat.

PRESENTATION AND GARNISH: dip the vegetables for garnish in salted boiling water for 30 seconds to heat through, then drain. Arrange the meat and sauce on heated serving plates and garnish on top and all around with the mixed miniature vegetables. Serve.

BRAISED SHIN OF VEAL WITH CARROT AND CORIANDER GARNISH

SERVES 4

2 veal shins
2 onions
2 cloves of garlic
2 leeks
2 celery sticks
2 carrots
1 bouquet garni
1 clove
15 g/½ oz salt

CARROT AND CORIANDER GARNISH
1 kg/2¼ lb carrots
2 tablespoons crushed coriander seeds
1 tablespoon olive oil
leaves from 1 sprig of thyme
1 clove of garlic, chopped
salt and pepper
150 ml/¼ pint cooking liquid from the veal

GARNISH
4 tablespoons chopped parsley

Preparation time: 20 minutes
Cooking time: 2-2½ hours

Braised Shin of Veal with Carrot and Coriander Garnish

TO PREPARE AND COOK THE VEAL: wash and peel the vegetables. Place them in a stockpot with the shins of veal and the remaining ingredients, cover with cold water, quickly bring to the boil, reduce the heat to a low boil and cook for 2-2½ hours, skimming off any scum that rises to the surface. The meat should be very tender.

TO PREPARE AND COOK THE CARROT AND CORIANDER GARNISH: peel the carrots and cut into julienne, about 5 mm/¼ inch wide. Heat the olive oil in a medium saucepan over a high heat. Add the carrots and the remaining ingredients (except for the veal cooking liquid) and stir constantly for 2 minutes. Pour in 150 ml/¼ pint veal cooking liquid, cover and cook for 3 more minutes.

GARNISH AND PRESENTATION: spread the carrot julienne on a serving dish and place the drained veal shins on top. Sprinkle with the chopped parsley and serve accompanied with coarse salt and mustard.

Note: you may freeze the remaining veal stock after sieving it and removing the fat. You can use this stock in recipes calling for chicken stock.

RAGOÛT OF SWEETBREADS 'ARCHIMBOLDO'

SERVES 2

225 g/8 oz calf's sweetbreads
15 g/½ oz dried morels
1 teaspoon olive oil (optional)
1 small bouquet garni (green part of a leek, parsley stalks,
sprig of thyme and sprig of rosemary)
½ carrot, coarsely chopped
¼ onion, coarsely chopped
1 tomato, quartered
2 tablespoons white wine
150 ml/¼ pint chicken stock made with a stock cube
100 g/4 oz white mushrooms, stalks removed, quartered
10 g/¼ oz shallot, chopped
salt and pepper
2 teaspoons truffle juice (available in cans or bottles)

VEGETABLE GARNISH
4 miniature carrots
4 miniature courgettes
4 miniature turnips
4 small asparagus spears
4 baby onions
15 g/½ oz fresh or frozen petits pois

TRUFFLE FLANS
1 egg
85 ml/3 fl oz stock from a pot-au-feu (or chicken stock)
50 ml/2 fl oz truffle juice (available in cans or bottles)
salt and pepper
10 g/¼ oz softened butter

GARNISH
sprigs of chervil
2 sprigs of thyme

Preparation time: about 50 minutes, plus 15 minutes the
night before
Cooking time: sweetbreads: 15 minutes; flans: 20 minutes

TO PREPARE THE SWEETBREADS THE NIGHT BEFORE: follow the direction on page 108 for soaking, blanching and weighting the sweetbreads. You should not skip this step, since unblanched sweetbreads would release their juices immediately into the sauce, making it less wholesome.

TO PREPARE THE VEGETABLE GARNISH: wash and peel the carrots, courgettes and turnips. Trim them with a knife to the size and shape of large olives. Scrape the asparagus and trim them to 6 cm/2½ inches long. Peel the onions. Defrost the *petits pois*, if frozen. Cook each vegetable separately in salted boiling water, until tender but still firm. Refresh under cold water to stop them from cooking further and place in a sieve so that you can reheat them at the last minute.

TO COOK THE SWEETBREADS: wash the morels, quarter, and soak for 30 minutes in lukewarm water.

Heat the olive oil in a small frying pan (or cut the fat content further by omitting it and using a nonstick saucepan). Add the sweetbreads, fry very gently on all sides just to colour, then add the bouquet garni, carrot, onion and tomato and fry gently for 5 minutes. Pour in the white wine, reduce by three-quarters to evaporate the alcohol and add the chicken stock. Cover and simmer for 10 minutes.

After 10 minutes, remove from the heat. With a slotted spoon, remove the sweetbreads and place on a plate. Pass the cooking liquid through a fine-mesh sieve and set aside.

TO PREPARE AND COOK THE TRUFFLE FLANS: preheat the oven to 140°C/275°F/Gas Mark 1. With a whisk, beat together in a bowl the egg, chicken stock and truffle juice and season with salt and pepper. Lightly grease 2 small ramekins (you may use espresso cups instead) with the softened butter and fill with the egg mixture. Place the ramekins in a baking tin and pour in hot water until it reaches half-way up the sides of the ramekins. Bake for 20 minutes.

TO FINISH THE SWEETBREADS: separate the sweetbreads into smaller sections, removing all remaining connective tissue. In a nonstick frying pan, quickly fry the white mushrooms, the soaked and drained morels, and chopped shallot. Season with salt and pepper and cook for 5 minutes.

Put the mushrooms, morels and sweetbreads in the saucepan used to cook the sweetbreads. Add the truffle juice and 85 ml/3 fl oz of the strained cooking liquid. Heat gently.

Dip the sieve of miniature vegetables in a saucepan of salted boiling water to heat through.

PRESENTATION AND GARNISH: on individual plates, arrange the heated sweetbread and mushroom mixture in a semi-circle on one side, using a slotted spoon, and the miniature vegetable garnish on the other. Unmould the flans on one edge of each plate by sliding a small knife around the edge of each flan. Pour some of the cooking liquid and truffle juice mixture over the sweetbreads and vegetables, garnish with chervil and pierce the top of each flan with a sprig of thyme.

TOMATOES STUFFED WITH VEAL, 'MÉMÉ MADELEINE'

SERVES 4

12 firm tomatoes, about 65 g/2½ oz each

STUFFING
300 g/11 oz lean veal (or skinless chicken breast)
2 potatoes, about 50 g/2 oz each
1 teaspoon olive oil
2 onions, chopped
1 clove of garlic, chopped
100 g/4 oz 0% fat fromage frais
4 tablespoons chopped parsley and chives
1 teaspoon reduced meat juices (see page 30)
salt and pepper

SAUCE
1 teaspoon olive oil
1 carrot, finely sliced
1 onion, finely sliced
1 clove of garlic, finely sliced
pulp from the tomatoes
3 tablespoons tomato purée
1 bouquet garni

300 ml/½ pint poultry stock (see page 31)
salt and pepper

Preparation time: 35-40 minutes
Cooking time: stuffing: 35 minutes; sauce: 20 minutes; tomatoes: 15 minutes

TO PREPARE THE TOMATOES: cut the top off each tomato and reserve. Scoop out the pulp with a small spoon and set aside. Place the tomatoes on a draining board, cut side down.

TO PREPARE THE STUFFING AND STUFF THE TOMATOES: steam the unpeeled potatoes for 25-30 minutes.

Heat the olive oil in a frying pan over a medium heat. Add the onions and garlic and fry gently until translucent and soft. Remove with a slotted spoon.

Finely chop the veal (or chicken) in a food processor.

When the potatoes are done, peel and mash with a fork in a bowl. Add the *fromage frais*, parsley and chives, fried garlic and onions, veal (or chicken), meat juice, salt and pepper. Mix with a wooden spatula or spoon until all the ingredients are well combined. Use a small spoon to stuff each tomato with some of the mixture. Cover with the reserved tops and place in a lightly oiled gratin or baking dish.

TO COOK THE SAUCE AND THE TOMATOES: Preheat the oven to 190°C/375°F/Gas Mark 5.

Heat the olive oil in a small saucepan. Add the carrot, onion and garlic and cook gently for 5 minutes until soft. Add the tomato pulp, tomato purée and bouquet garni. Cook for 2 minutes, stirring constantly.

Add the poultry stock and mix well. Simmer gently for 10 minutes. Remove the bouquet garni.

Transfer the sauce to a food processor and process for 30 seconds. Pass back into the saucepan through a fine-mesh sieve, correct the seasoning with salt and pepper and keep warm. Cook the tomatoes in the oven for 15 minutes.

PRESENTATION: when the tomatoes are cooked, pour a small ladleful of sauce on to each of 4 heated serving plates. Place 3 tomatoes on each plate and serve.

Lamb Sausages with Sage

LAMB SAUSAGES WITH SAGE

SERVES 4

400 g/14 oz lamb cut from the leg (skin, bone and
fat removed)
2 tablespoons chopped sage
130 cm/4 feet medium natural sausage casing (available
from a butcher's shop)
10 g/¼ oz salt
10 turns of the pepper mill
pinch of grated nutmeg
1 tablespoon olive oil

VEGETABLES
2 onions, finely chopped
2 carrots, finely chopped
1 clove of garlic, finely chopped
1 teaspoon olive oil
salt and pepper

SAUCE
100 ml/3½ fl oz water
150 ml/¼ pint veal stock (see page 33)
4-5 sage leaves

GARNISH
sage leaves

Preparation time: 25-30 minutes, plus 5 minutes the night
before
Cooking time: about 20 minutes

THE NIGHT BEFORE: cut the lamb into 2.5 cm/1 inch pieces, season with the salt, pepper and nutmeg and place in the refrigerator.

TO PREPARE THE LAMB AND THE VEGETABLES: the next day, heat the teaspoon of olive oil in a frying pan over a low heat. Add the onions, carrots and garlic and season with salt and pepper. Sweat gently, covered, for about 5 minutes. Transfer the mixture to a plate and leave to cool.

Chop the lamb coarsely in a meat mincer. In a large bowl, combine the meat, vegetables and chopped sage until thoroughly mixed.

TO PREPARE THE SAUSAGES: rinse the sausage casing by running cold water through it. Attach one end of the casing to the narrow end of a funnel or use a sausage maker, following the manufacturer's directions. Place some of the filling in the funnel and push through. Repeat until you have used up all the filling. Twist the filled casing at regular intervals to obtain 8 sausages of equal length. Separate the sausages by cutting between them with scissors.

TO COOK THE SAUSAGES: preheat the oven to 120°C/250°F/Gas Mark ½.

Prick each sausage several times with a fork. Heat the olive oil in a large, nonstick frying pan over a medium heat. Add the sausages and cook for about 8 minutes, browning them on all sides. Remove the sausages with a slotted spoon and keep warm in the oven.

TO COOK THE SAUCE: over a high heat, add the water to the pan the sausages were cooked in, deglaze by scraping the bottom with a wooden spoon and add the veal stock and sage leaves. Reduce for 3 minutes.

GARNISH AND PRESENTATION: arrange the sausages on warmed serving plates. Pour the sauce around them, garnish with sage leaves and serve. Accompany the sausages with Courgette Chips (see page 122).

ROSEMARY-ROASTED LAMB ON A VEGETABLE GALETTE

SERVES 4

2 loins of lamb (about 6-7 ribs each), or 1 large saddle of lamb, as much fat removed as possible (ask your butcher to do this)
large sprig of rosemary
1 clove of garlic, peeled
1 teaspoon olive oil
salt and pepper

VEGETABLES
250 g/9 oz mushrooms
500 g/1 ¼ lb fresh spinach
1 shallot, chopped
1 teaspoon olive oil
1 clove of garlic peeled
salt and pepper
pinch of nutmeg

SAUCE
150 ml/¼ pint veal stock (see page 33)
sprig of rosemary
1 clove of garlic, peeled and quartered
1 teaspoon cornflour
1 tablespoon cold water
salt and pepper

Preparation time: 30-35 minutes

Cooking time: lamb: 15-20 minutes if using loins; 30-40 minutes if using saddle; vegetables: 10-12 minutes

TO PREPARE THE LAMB: strip the leaves from the sprig of rosemary and chop. Rub the lamb with the garlic clove and then with the olive oil. Roll the lamb in the chopped rosemary and season with salt and pepper. Set aside.

TO PREPARE THE VEGETABLES: make a *duxelles* from the mushrooms, following the recipe on page 130. Set aside. Remove the stems from the spinach and rinse well. Peel and finely chop the shallot.

Heat half the olive oil in a saucepan over a medium heat. Add the chopped shallot and fry gently for 2-3 minutes until barely coloured. Raise the heat, add the spinach and the clove of garlic and cook, stirring constantly, until the leaves have wilted and any liquid has evaporated. Remove from the heat, remove and discard the garlic, season with salt, pepper and nutmeg. Set aside.

TO COOK THE LAMB: preheat the oven to 220°C/425°F/Gas Mark 7. Roast the lamb for 15-20 minutes, turning it half-way through the cooking time. (If using a saddle of lamb, allow about 30-40 minutes, depending on how well done you like it.) When the lamb is cooked, remove from the oven, cover with foil and let it rest in a warm place for about 10 minutes.

TO PREPARE THE SAUCE: place the veal stock, sprig of rosemary and garlic in a saucepan. Bring to the boil. Cook for 2 minutes, remove from the heat and set aside for 5 minutes so that the flavours mingle. Bring to the boil again, add the cornflour dissolved in the cold water, and boil, stirring constantly, for 2 minutes. Pass through a fine-mesh sieve into a saucepan and keep warm.

PRESENTATION: gently reheat the spinach and the mushroom *duxelles*. Carve the lamb away from the bone with a sharp knife and cut the meat into thin slices. Keep warm.

Place a metal ring 11 cm/4½ inches wide and 2.5 cm/1 inch high on each of 4 heated serving plates. Place a layer of the spinach in each ring and lightly press down. Cover with a layer of mushroom *duxelles* and top with lamb slices, arranging them like the petals of a flower. Remove the metal rings, pour the warm sauce round the meat and serve.

Note: you can accompany this dish with Baked Whole Garlic Cloves (see page 128) or a seasonal vegetable.

Rosemary-Roasted Lamb on a Vegetable Galette

VEGETABLES AND VEGETARIAN DISHES

VEGETABLE MEDLEY WITH HERB CREAM

SERVES 4

12 pickling onions
2 carrots
2 turnips
1 courgette
2 tomatoes, peeled, seeded and quartered
100 g/4 oz French beans
50 g/2 oz fresh or frozen petits pois
50 g/2 oz canned sweetcorn

HERB CREAM
25 g/1 oz skimmed milk powder
150 ml/¼ pint cooking liquid from the vegetables
1 tablespoon cornflour
1 tablespoon cold water
pinch of nutmeg
salt and pepper
6 tablespoons chopped fines herbes
(chervil, parsley, chives and tarragon)

GARNISH
sprigs of chervil, parsley, chives and tarragon

Preparation time: 25-30 minutes
Cooking time: vegetables: about 16 minutes altogether; herb cream: 5-6 minutes

TO PREPARE AND COOK THE VEGETABLES: peel and wash all the vegetables, shell fresh *petits pois* or defrost frozen ones. Drain the sweetcorn.

Cook the pickling onions in salted boiling water for 10 minutes. Drain and refresh under cold water. Cut the carrots, turnips and courgette in slices 3 mm/⅛ inch thick.

Place the French beans in a large saucepan of salted boiling water and cook for 3 minutes after the water has returned to the boil. Add the carrots and turnips and cook for 2 minutes more. Add the sliced courgette and tomato and cook for 1 minute more. The total cooking time for the vegetables should be 6-7 minutes; they should still be firm. Drain in a colander, reserving 150 ml/¼ pint cooking liquid, and refresh under cold water.

TO PREPARE THE HERB CREAM: dissolve the milk powder in the reserved cooking liquid and bring to the boil. Add the cornflour, dissolved in the cold water, and cook for 1 minute, beating constantly with a wire whisk. Remove from the heat and season with the nutmeg, salt and pepper. Add the cooked vegetables, sweetcorn and peas. Place over a low heat and heat for 4 minutes.

PRESENTATION: just before serving, add the chopped herbs to the mixture and mix well. Serve the vegetable medley in a heated serving dish or on 4 heated individual serving plates, garnished with the sprigs of herbs.

SAUTÉED POTATOES

SERVES 4

500 g/1 ¼ lb firm, waxy potatoes, peeled
1 clove of garlic
sprig of thyme
1 tablespoon olive oil
1 bay leaf
2 tablespoons chopped parsley
salt and pepper

Preparation time: 10-15 minutes
Cooking time: 7 minutes

TO PREPARE THE POTATOES: cut into 5 mm/¼ inch dice. Rinse in cold water and dry with a tea towel.

Peel the garlic clove and cut in 2. Rub the thyme between your fingers to release the leaves from the stem.

TO COOK THE POTATOES: heat the oil over a high heat in a large nonstick frying pan. Add the potatoes and toss gently in the oil for 1 minute. Lower the heat, add the garlic, thyme, bay leaf and season with salt and pepper and, stirring often, cook the potatoes for 5-6 minutes, or until golden brown.

GARNISH AND PRESENTATION: when the potatoes are cooked, remove the garlic and bay leaf and discard. Add the chopped parsley and toss gently. Transfer the potatoes to a heated platter and serve.

COURGETTE CHIPS

SERVES 4

2 long, narrow courgettes
1 clove of garlic
salt

Preparation time: 5 minutes
Cooking time: 10 minutes

TO PREPARE THE COURGETTES: slice the courgettes into rounds about 3 mm/⅛ inch thick. Moisten some kitchen paper with the olive oil. Peel the garlic clove and push it on to the tines of a fork.

TO COOK THE CHIPS: heat 2 large, nonstick frying pans over a high heat. When they are very hot, grease them with the oil-moistened kitchen paper (being careful not to touch the pan with your fingers). Rub each pan with the garlic clove.

Reduce the heat and arrange the courgette rounds in the frying pans so that they don't overlap. Cook for 3 minutes on each side. They should be quite dry and golden without being too darkly coloured.

When they are cooked, transfer them to a rack in a warm oven until you are ready to serve them.

PRESENTATION: arrange the chips on a platter and sprinkle with salt.

BRAISED FENNEL

SERVES 4

1 kg/2 ¼ lb fennel bulbs
bunch of dill
1 tablespoon olive oil
85 ml/3 fl oz water
salt and pepper

Preparation time: 4 minutes
Cooking time: 15 minutes

TO PREPARE THE FENNEL: wash the fennel bulbs and trim by slicing off the bottom and removing the toughest outer leaves and the darker green stems. Cut each bulb lengthwise into thin slices. Remove the stems from the dill and chop the leaves finely; set aside.

TO COOK THE FENNEL: heat the oil in a heavy-bottomed saucepan over a high heat. Add the fennel and cook gently to soften for 2 minutes, stirring constantly with a wooden spoon.

Add the water, salt and pepper, cover and cook over a low heat for about 12 minutes.

PRESENTATION: remove the fennel from the saucepan with a slotted spoon, arrange on a serving dish and sprinkle with the chopped dill.

BROCCOLI PURÉE

SERVES 4

750 g/1 ¾ lb broccoli
2 tablespoons skimmed milk powder
100 ml/3 ½ fl oz water
salt and pepper

Preparation time: 10 minutes
Cooking time: 6-8 minutes

TO PREPARE AND COOK THE BROCCOLI: wash the broccoli. Trim the bottoms of the stems and cut off the florets. Peel the stems with a vegetable peeler and cut in 4 lengthwise.

Bring a saucepan of salted water to the boil. Add the broccoli, both florets and stems, and cook for 6-8 minutes. Drain.

FINISHING THE PURÉE AND PRESENTATION: dissolve the milk powder in the water. Place the broccoli in a food processor and process for 1 minute; add the milk and process again for 30 seconds until smooth. Correct the seasoning with salt and pepper. Transfer the purée to the top part of a double boiler and keep warm.

When ready to serve, pour the purée into a heated dish or place on individual serving plates with the main course.

CARROT PURÉE

SERVES 4

750 g/1¾ lb carrots
1 onion
1 clove of garlic
1 teaspoon olive oil
1 bay leaf
sprig of thyme
300 ml/½ pint water
salt and pepper

Preparation time: 10 minutes
Cooking time: 20 minutes

TO PREPARE AND COOK THE CARROTS: peel and wash the carrots, onion and garlic. Slice them into thin rounds. Heat the oil in a medium saucepan over a low heat. Add the carrots, onion and garlic and cook very gently, covered, for about 5-6 minutes, stirring occasionally.

Add the bay leaf, thyme, water and salt to taste. Cover the carrots with a round of greaseproof paper. Put a plate on top of the paper and, finally, top with the lid of the pan. Cook over a low heat for 15 minutes.

FINISHING THE PURÉE AND PRESENTATION: When the carrots are tender, remove the thyme and bay leaf and transfer the contents of the saucepan to a food processor. Process until smooth.

Pour the purée into the top part of a double boiler, correct the seasoning with salt and pepper and keep warm.

When ready to serve, pour the carrot purée into a heated serving dish or place on individual serving plates with the main course.

CELERIAC AND POTATO PURÉE

SERVES 4

500 g/1¼ lb celeriac
200 g/7 oz potatoes
1 litre/1¾ pints skimmed milk
salt and pepper
pinch of nutmeg

Preparation time: 10 minutes
Cooking time: 20 minutes

TO PREPARE THE VEGETABLES: peel and wash the celeriac and the potatoes. Cut into pieces and place in a saucepan with the milk and salt. Bring to the boil and simmer for 20 minutes.

TO FINISH THE PURÉE AND PRESENTATION: drain the vegetables in a colander set over a bowl. Place the vegetables in a food processor. Add about 175 ml/6 fl oz cooking liquid and process until smooth, making sure the purée is neither too thick nor too thin. Pour into a saucepan and heat over a very low heat. Correct the seasoning with salt and pepper and a pinch of nutmeg. Serve in a heated dish.

Note: you may reheat any leftover purée by transferring it to a greased gratin dish and placing in a hot oven.

Carrot Purée, Celeriac and Potato Purée and Chick Pea Purée

CHICK PEA PURÉE WITH CUMIN

SERVES 4

100 g/4 oz dried chick peas
1 teaspoon olive oil
1 onion, chopped
½ clove of garlic, chopped
1 teaspoon powdered cumin
salt and pepper

GARNISH
1 tablespoon chopped flat-leaf parsley
1 tablespoon chopped coriander

Preparation time: 5 minutes, plus soaking overnight
Cooking time: about 50 minutes

TO PREPARE AND COOK THE CHICK PEAS: soak the chick peas overnight in a large quantity of cold water.

The next day, drain the chick peas, rinse under cold water and place in a saucepan of fresh water. Simmer, uncovered, for about 45 minutes. The chick peas should be completely covered in water during this time (add more water if too much has evaporated) and should be tender when cooked. Drain in a colander set over a bowl and reserve the liquid.

TO PREPARE THE PURÉE: place the chick peas in a food processor, add a small amount of the cooking liquid and process until smooth. Set aside.

Heat the oil in a saucepan over a low heat. Add the onion and garlic and cook gently until soft, about 3 minutes. Add the cumin, mix well and cook for 1 more minute.

Add the chick pea purée to the saucepan. Season with salt and pepper and heat over a low heat for 2-3 minutes, stirring with a wooden spatula so that the purée does not stick to the bottom of the pan.

PRESENTATION: pour the purée into a heated dish and sprinkle with the parsley and coriander.

Note: the dish is rich in protein.

BOULANGÈRE POTATOES

SERVES 4

300 g/11 oz firm, waxy potatoes
3 onions
1 clove of garlic
1 teaspoon olive oil
salt and pepper
sprig of thyme
½ bay leaf
400 ml/14 fl oz vegetable or poultry stock (see page 31) or
water

GARNISH
2 tablespoons chopped parsley

Preparation time: 25 minutes
Cooking time: about 1 hour

TO PREPARE THE VEGETABLES: peel and wash the potatoes and onions.

Cut the potatoes into slices 5 mm/¼ inch thick and rinse in cold water. Drain on a tea towel. Slice the onions very finely and peel and quarter the garlic clove.

TO COOK THE POTATOES: preheat the oven to 190°C/375°F/Gas Mark 5.

Heat the oil in a frying pan over a medium heat. Add the onions and garlic and cook gently for 5-6 minutes, until soft and golden. Season with salt.

Meanwhile, layer the potato slices in a gratin dish and season with salt and pepper. Sprinkle with the thyme rubbed between the fingers and the bay leaf, crushed into tiny pieces.

When the onions are golden, spread them on top of the potatoes and add the poultry stock or water. Cover with a sheet of foil and bake for about 1 hour, checking them from time to time.

At the end of an hour or so, the liquid should have evaporated. If not, remove the foil shortly before the potatoes are cooked.

PRESENTATION: remove the gratin dish from the oven, sprinkle with the chopped parsley and serve immediately.

Note: you can prepare the same dish using turnips or celeriac, both of which are lower in calories.

ARTICHOKE HEARTS À BLANC

SERVES 4

4 large globe artichokes
1 lemon
1 tablespoon plain flour
900 ml/1 ½ pints water
1 teaspoon salt

Preparation time: 3 minutes
Cooking time: 20 minutes

TO PREPARE THE ARTICHOKES: snap off the stems from the artichokes and remove the outermost leaves. With a serrated knife, cut off 5 cm/2 inches from the tops of the leaves. Then, with a knife, trim round the base and the choke, removing the lower leaves. Rub the artichokes with the cut side of half the lemon.

TO COOK THE ARTICHOKES: put the flour, water, juice from the lemon, and salt in a saucepan and beat well to dissolve the flour. Add the artichokes, cover with greaseproof paper and put the lid on the pan. Bring to a gentle boil over a medium heat and cook for about 20 minutes. The artichoke hearts should still be quite firm.

PRESENTATION: cool the artichokes and remove the choke with a teaspoon. Keep the artichoke hearts in their cooking liquid. Drain well before serving, either plain with a main course or simply with a little light vinaigrette (see page 36).

GRATIN OF COURGETTES AND ONIONS

SERVES 4

750 g/1 ¾ lb courgettes
400 g/14 oz onions
bunch of thyme or 2-3 basil leaves
250 ml/8 fl oz water
50 g/2 oz skimmed milk powder
salt and pepper
pinch of mace

Preparation time: 15-20 minutes
Cooking time: 1 ½ hours

TO COOK THE VEGETABLES: peel the courgettes and onions and cut into 3 mm/⅛ inch slices.

Bring 2 saucepans of salted water to the boil. Plunge one vegetable into each saucepan. As soon as the water comes back to the boil, drain the vegetables in separate colanders. Leave to cool for 5 minutes.

TO PREPARE THE SAUCE: remove the leaves from the thyme, or chop the basil finely. Warm the water and add the milk powder, thyme or basil, salt and pepper and mace. Whisk to blend, then set aside.

TO PREPARE AND COOK THE GRATIN: preheat the oven to 190°C/375°F/Gas Mark 4.

Arrange the onions and courgettes in alternate layers in a gratin dish. Pour on the milk mixture and bake for 1 ½ hours.

If the gratin becomes too brown on the top during cooking, cover it with foil.

PRESENTATION: serve in the cooking dish, cut into neat portions, to accompany meat or fish, served on individual plates.

BAKED WHOLE GARLIC CLOVES

SERVES 4

40 cloves of garlic
500 ml/17 fl oz water
1 tablespoon olive oil
½ teaspoon coarse salt

Preparation time: 10-15 minutes
Cooking time: 30 minutes

TO PREPARE THE GARLIC: detach the cloves from the heads of garlic and, without peeling them, remove the loose, paper-like exterior skin.

TO COOK THE GARLIC: preheat the oven to 180°C/350°F/Gas Mark 4.
   Place the garlic in a sauté pan and pour in the water and oil. Add the salt and bring to the boil over a high heat. Remove the pan, cover with a sheet of greaseproof paper and bake in the oven for 30 minutes.

PRESENTATION: remove the pan from the oven and transfer the garlic and cooking juices to a dish. Cool for 10 minutes.
   Peel the garlic, being careful not to crush the cloves. Place in a small ovenproof dish and heat for 5 minutes before serving as an accompaniment to meat or fish.

Note: you may also add the cooked garlic cloves to the dish they are accompanying during the final 2-3 minutes of cooking.

EASY ONION CONFIT

SERVES 4

1 kg/2 ¼ lb onions
2 tablespoons olive oil
2 bay leaves
coarse salt and freshly ground pepper

Preparation time: 10 minutes
Cooking time: 2 ½-3 hours

TO PREPARE THE ONIONS: without actually peeling the onions, remove the dry, outermost layer of skin by rubbing between the fingers.
   Pour the oil into a bowl and add the onions. Toss to coat.

TO COOK THE ONIONS: preheat the oven to 190°/375°/Gas Mark 5.
   Place the onions in a casserole with the bay leaves. Cover and bake for 2 ½-3 hours. From time to time, check that they are not cooking too fast and reduce the heat if necessary.

PRESENTATION: remove the onions from the oven and make an incision in the top of each one with a pair of scissors. Squeeze them open slightly. Place on a serving dish and serve with coarse salt and a pepper mill on the side.

Note: you can bake large shallots in the same way, reducing the cooking time to about 1 ½ hours.

PRUNE AND TURNIP CONSERVE

SERVES 4

750 g/1 ¾ lb turnips
100 g/4 oz prunes
1 clove of garlic
1 tablespoon olive oil
1 bay leaf
salt and pepper
100 ml/3 ½ oz veal stock (see page 33)

Preparation time: 15-20 minutes
Cooking time: about 15 minutes

TO PREPARE THE TURNIPS AND PRUNES: peel the turnips and cut them into 3mm/⅛ inch slices. Stone the prunes and cut them into small cubes. Peel the garlic.

TO COOK THE CONSERVE: plunge the slices of turnip into a saucepan of boiling water for 2 minutes. Drain.

In a nonstick pan, heat the oil until it starts to smoke. Add the slices of turnip, the whole garlic clove and the bay leaf. Sauté for 4 minutes, turning with a spatula.

Lower the heat, then add the small pieces of prunes, salt and pepper, and mix together well. Continue cooking for 1 minute. Moisten with the veal stock, turning and scraping the bottom of the pan. Season and leave, uncovered, to reduce for a good 2 minutes.

FINISHING AND PRESENTATION: remove the garlic and bay leaf. Pour into a warmed dish and serve.

STIR-FRIED BEANSPROUTS WITH SOY SAUCE

SERVES 4

400 g/14 oz fresh soya beansprouts
1 tablespoon soy sauce, plus extra for serving
1 large carrot, about 200 g/7 oz
10 g/¼ oz fresh root ginger
1 teaspoon dark or light sesame oil
salt and pepper
1 teaspoon red wine vinegar

GARNISH
3 tablespoons chopped coriander

Preparation time: 10 minutes
Cooking time: 5 minutes

TO PREPARE THE VEGETABLES: rinse the beansprouts and drain well. Peel and wash the carrot and cut into a coarse julienne. Peel the ginger and chop. Set aside.

TO COOK THE VEGETABLES: heat the sesame oil over a high heat in a large nonstick frying pan. Add the beansprouts, carrot and ginger. Fry for 4 minutes, stirring constantly with a wooden spatula. Season lightly with salt and pepper.

PRESENTATION: remove the frying pan from the heat, add the vinegar and soy sauce and toss. Correct the seasoning with salt and pepper, if necessary. Place on a heated platter, sprinkle with the chopped coriander and serve with a small bowl of soy sauce on the side.

MUSHROOMS STUFFED WITH MUSHROOM DUXELLES

SERVES 4

750 g/1¾ lb large white mushrooms
100 ml/3½ fl oz water
salt and pepper
juice of ¼ lemon
1 teaspoon olive oil
½ clove of garlic, finely chopped
1 onion, finely chopped
1 teaspoon curry powder
4 tablespoons chopped parsley
2 tablespoons skimmed milk powder

Preparation time: 15 minutes
Cooking time: about 25 minutes

TO PREPARE THE MUSHROOMS: trim the mushroom stalks and wash carefully. Separate the caps from the stalks.

Choose the 12 largest caps and place in a saucepan with the water, salt and lemon juice. Cover, bring to the boil and cook for 6-7 minutes over a high heat. With a slotted spoon, remove the mushrooms and place on some kitchen paper, stalk end down. Leave the cooking liquid in the pan.

TO PREPARE THE DUXELLES: chop the remaining mushroom caps and stalks and place in the saucepan that was used for cooking the large caps. Cook over a high heat until all the liquid has evaporated. Transfer to a food processor and chop coarsely.

Heat the olive oil in a saucepan and add the garlic, onion and curry powder. Sweat gently for 3 minutes. Add the chopped mushrooms, parsley, skimmed milk powder, salt and pepper and mix well.

GARNISH AND PRESENTATION: heat the oven to 190°C/375°F/Gas Mark 5.

Using a spoon, stuff the large mushroom caps with the *duxelles*. Arrange the caps in a baking dish and bake for 10 minutes. Serve from the dish.

RICE PILAF

SERVES 4

120 g/4½ oz long-grain rice
1 teaspoon olive oil
small piece of garlic, chopped (optional)
1 onion, chopped
sprig of parsley
sprig of thyme
½ bay leaf
85 ml/3 fl oz white wine
½ vegetable or chicken stock cube dissolved in 300 ml/ ½ pint water
salt

Preparation time: 5 minutes
Cooking time: about 25 minutes

COOKING AND PRESENTATION: heat the olive oil in a saucepan over a low heat. Add the garlic (if using), onion, parsley, thyme and bay leaf. Cook gently for 3 minutes until soft. Add the rice. Fry, stirring constantly, for 2 minutes.

Add the white wine and chicken stock and season with salt. Bring to the boil over a high heat, stirring.

Lower the heat, cover and simmer until all the liquid has been absorbed (about 18 minutes). When the rice is cooked, transfer immediately to a heated dish or serve on individual plates next to the main course.

VEGETARIAN MAIN COURSES

VEGETABLE AND TOFU 'LASAGNE'

SERVES 4

400 g/14 oz firm tofu
400 g/14 oz carrots
100 g/4 oz turnips
200 g/7 oz celeriac
200 g/7 oz potatoes
300 g/11 oz courgettes
1 tablespoon salt
500 g/1 ¼ lb spinach

VEGETABLE BINDING
bunch of sage
200 ml/7 fl oz water
1 clove of garlic, chopped
2 tablespoons cornflour
2 tablespoons cold water
pinch of nutmeg
3 egg whites
salt and pepper

PARSLEY SAUCE
bunch of parsley
200 ml/7 fl oz vegetable stock
1 tablespoon cornflour
1 tablespoon cold water
salt and pepper
1 tablespoon skimmed milk powder

Preparation time: 30 minutes
Cooking time: vegetables: about 10 minutes altogether;
'lasagne': 25 minutes

TO PREPARE THE VEGETABLES: wash and peel the vegetables. Cut the carrots, turnips, celeriac, potatoes and courgettes into slices 3 mm/¹/₈ inch thick. Bring 2.75 litres/4³/₄ pints water and the salt to the boil in a large saucepan. Blanch each vegetable (except the potatoes) separately in the boiling water for 1-3 minutes, keeping them firm. Remove with a slotted spoon and place, separately, on tea towels to drain.

Place the potatoes in a saucepan of cold salted water. Bring to the boil and drain after 3-4 minutes. Put 2 tablespoons cold water into a saucepan, add the spinach and wilt the leaves for 1 minute over a high heat until the water has evaporated. Place on a tea towel to drain.

TO PREPARE THE VEGETABLE BINDING: take a small handful of sage leaves from the bunch and chop very coarsely. Boil the water, sage and garlic in a pan, uncovered, for 2 minutes. Add the cornflour, dissolved in the cold water, and the nutmeg and boil for 1 minute more. Remove from the heat and cool for 5 minutes. Beat in the egg whites.

TO FINISH THE VEGETABLES: place each vegetable in a shallow bowl. Divide the vegetable binding between them and season with salt and pepper. Carefully mix to coat the vegetables.

TO PREPARE AND COOK THE 'LASAGNE': preheat the oven to 190°C/375°F/Gas Mark 5.

Lightly oil a 20 cm/8 inch square cake tin. Cut the tofu into slices 5 mm/¹/₄ inch thick. Beginning with the tofu, arrange alternate layers of vegetables and tofu in the cake tin. Bake in the oven for 25 minutes.

TO PREPARE AND COOK THE PARSLEY SAUCE: remove the stalks from the parsley and chop finely. In a small saucepan, boil the stock and parsley for 1 minute. Add the cornflour, dissolved in the cold water, and boil for 1 minute more. Season with salt and pepper and keep warm over a very low heat.

PRESENTATION: When the 'lasagne' is cooked, turn out on to a board and cut into 4 slices. Place on 4 heated serving plates.

Place the hot parsley sauce in a food processor, add the milk powder and process for 15 seconds. Pour the parsley sauce over the 'lasagne' slices and serve.

CARROT FLANS WITH CARROT AND COURGETTE GARNISH

SERVES 4

500 g/1 ¼ lb young carrots
500 ml/17 fl oz vegetable stock
sprig of thyme
½ bay leaf
1 clove of garlic, coarsely chopped
200 g/7 oz tofu
3 egg whites
salt and pepper
10 g/¼ oz margarine

CARROT AND COURGETTE GARNISH

750 g/1 ¾ lb carrots
1 large courgette, about 350 g/12 oz
175 ml/6 fl oz white wine
1 teaspoon olive oil
4 sprigs of parsley
salt and pepper

Preparation time: 30-35 minutes
Cooking time: flans: 10 minutes; carrots: 8 minutes;
julienne: 1 minute

TO PREPARE THE FLANS: peel all the carrots required for the dish. Take 500 g/1¼ lb and slice them into thin rounds. Place in a saucepan with the stock, thyme, bay leaf and garlic. Bring to the boil and cook, covered, for about 10 minutes.

When the carrots are cooked, drain over a saucepan to retain the cooking liquid. Remove the thyme and bay leaf.

Place the carrots, tofu (cut into pieces), egg whites and salt and pepper in a food processor. Process for 40 seconds until smooth. Grease 4 individual ramekins with the margarine. Fill with the carrot purée.

TO PREPARE THE CARROT AND COURGETTE GARNISH: take 400 g/14 oz of the remaining carrots. Cut into 4 cm/1½ inch pieces and halve each piece on the diagonal. Place in the saucepan of reserved cooking liquid. If the liquid does not cover the carrots, add some more stock or water. Wash the courgette, trim the ends and cut into medium julienne. Julienne the remaining whole carrots as well. Set aside.

TO COOK THE FLANS AND THE GARNISH: preheat the oven to 190°C/375°F/Gas Mark 5.

Place the ramekins in a baking dish and add enough simmering water to come two-thirds of the way up the sides of the ramekins. Bake in the oven for about 10 minutes.

Meanwhile, bring the diagonally cut carrots to the boil in the reserved cooking liquid. Cook for about 8 minutes. Remove from the heat and set aside in the liquid.

Reduce the white wine in a saucepan over a high heat. Meanwhile, unmould the flans on 4 heated serving plates and keep warm.

When the white wine has reduced by half, add the olive oil and 2-3 tablespoons carrot cooking liquid. Correct the seasoning if necessary. Add the carrot and courgette julienne and stir with a fork over a high heat for 1 minute.

PRESENTATION: surround the flans with the vegetable julienne and the drained, cooked carrots. Garnish with the sprigs of parsley and serve.

Carrot Flans with Carrot and Courgette Garnish

VEGETABLE POT-AU-FEU WITH CINNAMON AND HARISSA

SERVES 4

4 small white onions
4 red onions
8 cloves of garlic
100 g/4 oz frozen petits pois
4 carrots
4 leeks
1 celery heart
½ cauliflower
100 g/4 oz French beans
2 courgettes
4 tomatoes
1 bouquet garni
1 piece of cinnamon stick, 5 cm/2 inches long
½ teaspoon harissa (see note right)
coarse salt and freshly ground pepper

Preparation time: 20-25 minutes
Cooking time: 20 minutes

TO PREPARE THE VEGETABLES: wash and trim both kinds of onion and the garlic. Do not peel. Place in a large saucepan of boiling water and cook for 20 minutes.

Defrost the *petits pois*. Peel the carrots and leave them whole. Remove and discard the green part and the stem end of the leeks, cut a cross into the pale green part and wash well. Wash the celery heart. Wash the cauliflower and divide into 4 large florets. Trim the beans. Peel the courgettes and quarter lengthwise. Dip the tomatoes into boiling water for 30 seconds, peel, quarter and seed.

TO COOK THE POT-AU-FEU: bring a large saucepan of salted water to the boil. Add the carrots, celery, leeks, bouquet garni and cinnamon stick. When the water returns to the boil, cook for 5 minutes. Add the cauliflower and cook for 10 minutes. Finally, add the French beans and courgettes. Boil for 4 minutes longer, then remove from the heat. Add the *harissa* and 1 litre/1¾ pints of the onion cooking water. Cover the saucepan and keep warm.

GARNISH AND PRESENTATION: remove the onions and garlic from their cooking liquid with a slotted spoon. Refresh in cold water, peel carefully and add to the other vegetables. Add the peas and tomato quarters and heat over a high heat for 1 minute. Place the vegetables in a serving dish. Pour their cooking liquid into a soup tureen and serve. Pass around small dishes of coarse salt and a pepper mill.

Note: *harissa* is a condiment from North Africa and the Middle East. It is a purée made from small peppers, cayenne, oil, garlic and coriander, pounded with cumin and dried mint or verbena leaves.

Vegetable Pot-au-Feu with Cinnamon and Harissa

TAGLIATELLE WITH FRESH TOMATO AND THYME SAUCE

SERVES 4

250 g/9 oz tagliatelle

SAUCE

8 ripe tomatoes
2 sprigs of thyme
3 tablespoons flat-leaf parsley
2 tablespoons olive oil
¼ clove of garlic, chopped
salt and pepper

Preparation time: 10 minutes
Cooking time: pasta: 5-10 minutes, depending on brand used; sauce: 1 minute

TO PREPARE THE SAUCE: dip the tomatoes into boiling water for 30 seconds. Refresh under cold water, peel, halve and seed. Cut the tomatoes into small cubes and set aside in a sieve set over a bowl.

Remove and discard the stems from the parsley and chop the leaves very coarsely. Set aside. Heat the olive oil in a saucepan over a high heat, add the chopped garlic and the thyme, rubbed between the fingers to release the leaves. After 30 seconds, add the tomato cubes. Season with salt and pepper and keep warm over a very low heat.

TO COOK THE PASTA: cook the tagliatelle in a large pan of salted boiling water, according to the instructions on the packet.

PRESENTATION: drain the tagliatelle and divide between 4 heated serving plates. Add the parsley to the tomato sauce and raise the heat until the sauce is very hot. Toss the pasta with the sauce and serve immediately.

WHOLEWHEAT SPAGHETTI WITH GARLIC AND BASIL

SERVES 4

250 g/9 oz wholewheat spaghetti
3 cloves of garlic
1 bunch of basil
4 tablespoons olive oil
salt and pepper

GARNISH

sprigs of basil

Preparation time: 5 minutes
Cooking time: about 15 minutes

TO COOK THE SPAGHETTI: cook the spaghetti in a large saucepan of salted boiling water for about 15 minutes, or until just *al dente*.

Crush the unpeeled cloves of garlic with the flat side of a large knife. In a small saucepan, heat the olive oil and garlic over a high heat for 1½ minutes. Reduce the heat.

Set aside 4 sprigs of basil. Remove and discard the stems from the bunch; chop the leaves and set aside.

GARNISH AND PRESENTATION: when the pasta is cooked, drain and return to the saucepan.

Pass the olive oil through a fine-mesh sieve over the spaghetti, add the chopped basil and toss quickly. Correct the seasoning with salt and pepper.

Divide the pasta between 4 heated shallow bowls or serving plates. Garnish with the basil sprigs. Serve immediately.

Note: you can serve freshly grated Parmesan cheese with this pasta dish.

Wholewheat Spaghetti with Garlic and Basil

dESSERTS

VANILLA-FLAVOURED APRICOT COMPOTE

SERVES 4

500 g/1 ¼ lb fresh apricots
1 vanilla pod
100 ml/3 ½ fl oz water
8-12 teaspoons Nutrasweet sweetener (according to taste)

DECORATION
225 g/8 oz strawberries
4 sprigs of mint

Preparation time: 10 minutes
Cooking time: 8 minutes

TO PREPARE THE APRICOTS: wash, quarter and stone the apricots.

TO COOK THE COMPOTE: split the vanilla pod in half lengthwise. Place the apricots, vanilla pod and water in a saucepan. Bring to a simmer and cook, covered, for 8 minutes, stirring occasionally to prevent sticking.

When the compote is cooked, add the sweetener and mix. Remove the vanilla pod and, with a small knife, scrape the tiny black seeds into the compote. Stir, then leave to cool to room temperature.

DECORATION AND PRESENTATION: wash the strawberries and halve them lengthwise without removing the stalks. Divide the compote between 4 plates, surround with the halved strawberries and decorate with the mint and, if liked, pieces of vanilla pod. Serve at room temperature or ice cold.

Note: you can replace the apricots with peaches or apples. If you use apples, perk up their flavour by adding the juice of a lemon or lime to the compote.

MIRABELLE PLUMS WITH PEACH SOUFFLÉ

SERVES 4

150 g/5 oz mirabelle plums in syrup
2 very ripe peaches, about 100 g/4 oz each (or 2 canned peaches in syrup)
750 ml/1 ¼ pints water
75 g/3 oz Nutrasweet sweetener
1 vanilla pod
½ teaspoon peach brandy
2 egg yolks
20 g/¾ oz softened butter
7 egg whites

Preparation time: 15-20 minutes
Cooking time: peaches: about 7 minutes; soufflé: 8 minutes

TO PREPARE THE PEACHES: combine the water, 50 g/2 oz sweetener and the vanilla pod in a pan. Peel, quarter and stone the peaches, add to the pan and cook for about 7 minutes. Drain, remove the vanilla pod, then purée in a food processor with the remaining sweetener and peach brandy. Pour into a bowl, add the egg yolks and mix well. Use the softened butter to grease 4 individual soufflé dishes.

TO PREPARE THE SOUFFLÉ: Beat the egg whites with a whisk until stiff. Fold a quarter of the egg whites into the peach purée. Gently fold in the remaining egg whites with a wooden spatula.

COOKING AND PRESENTATION: preheat the oven to 190°C/375°F/Gas Mark 5.

Drain the mirabelle plums and divide between the 4 soufflé dishes. Fill with the soufflé mixture and smooth the surface with a palette knife or the flat side of a knife blade. Bake in the oven for 8 minutes. Remove from the oven, set each soufflé dish on a small plate and serve immediately.

RED BERRIES IN WINE ASPIC WITH RASPBERRY COULIS

SERVES 4

*500 g/1 ¼ lb mixed red berries (strawberries, raspberries,
redcurrants, blackcurrants and blackberries)*

ASPIC
250 ml/8 fl oz dry rosé wine
3 tablespoons powdered gelatine
5 teaspoons Nutrasweet sweetener
5 large mint leaves

RASPBERRY COULIS
150 g/5 oz raspberries
4 teaspoons Nutrasweet sweetener
juice of ½ lemon
2 tablespoons water

Preparation time: 20 minutes, plus at least 2 hours' chilling
Cooking time: 2 minutes

TO PREPARE THE BERRIES: wash and stem the berries and
place on a tea towel to dry.

TO PREPARE THE ASPIC: bring the wine to the boil and boil for
2 minutes to evaporate the alcohol. Dissolve the gelatine in
the wine and cool for 20 minutes. Add the sweetener and mix
together.

TO FINISH THE ASPIC: divide the berries between 4 small
ramekins. Snip the mint leaves into tiny pieces and sprinkle
over the fruit. Fill the ramekins with the liquid aspic and
place in the refrigerator for at least 2 hours.

TO PREPARE THE RASPBERRY COULIS: pick over the
raspberries, then place in a food processor with the
sweetener and lemon juice. Process for 20 seconds.
  Pass the coulis through a fine-mesh sieve into a bowl. Add
1-2 tablespoons water if it is too thick. Refrigerate.

PRESENTATION: dip the ramekins in hot water for 5 seconds,
then unmould on to 4 plates. Pour the coulis around the
aspics, covering the plates. Serve immediately.

POACHED PEARS WITH BLACKCURRANT SAUCE

SERVES 4

4 William pears, about 200 g/7 oz each, not too ripe
200 g/7 oz fresh or frozen blackcurrants
750 ml/1 ¼ pints water
juice of 1 lemon
1 clove
1 small stick of cinnamon
12 teaspoons Nutrasweet sweetener

Preparation time: 7-10 minutes
Cooking time: 10-20 minutes

TO PREPARE THE BLACKCURRANT SAUCE: lightly crush the
blackcurrants and place in a saucepan with the water, lemon
juice, clove and cinnamon. Bring to the boil.

TO PREPARE AND COOK THE PEARS: peel the pears with a
vegetable peeler, keeping the stalks intact.
  Place the pears in the pan of blackcurrants and simmer
for 10-20 minutes depending on the pears' size and ripeness.
When they are tender, place the pears in a bowl. Dissolve the
sweetener in the blackcurrant sauce and pass through a fine-
mesh sieve on to the pears, pressing on the blackcurrants to
release all the juice. Place the pears and sauce in the
refrigerator.

PRESENTATION: serve the pears, surrounded by the
blackcurrant sauce, on individual plates.

EARL GREY TEA CUSTARDS WITH LEMON SAUCE

SERVES 4

2 tablespoons Earl Grey tea (or 3 tea bags)
500 ml/17 fl oz skimmed milk
6 egg whites
12 teaspoons Nutrasweet sweetener

LEMON SAUCE
100 g/4 oz 0% fat fromage frais
juice of 2 lemons and 1 orange
6 teaspoons Nutrasweet sweetener

DECORATION
100 g/4 oz raspberries

Preparation time: 10 minutes
Cooking time: 25 minutes, 2½ hours before serving

TO PREPARE AND COOK THE CUSTARDS: preheat the oven to 180°C/350°F/Gas Mark 4. Heat the milk until barely simmering, add the tea and simmer for 1 minute. Remove from the heat and steep for 10 minutes.

Place the egg whites in a bowl and beat for 20 seconds, gradually adding the sweetener. Pass the milk through a fine-mesh sieve into the egg whites. Mix with a wooden spoon and remove the foam that rises to the surface with a small spoon.

Pour the liquid into 4 small individual ramekin dishes. Place in a simmering *bain-marie* and bake in the oven for 25 minutes. To test if they are ready, gently shake the dishes: if the surface trembles, the custards are done.

Remove the custards from the *bain-marie* and leave to cool first at room temperature for 15 minutes, then in the refrigerator for at least 2 hours.

TO PREPARE THE LEMON SAUCE: place the ingredients for the sauce in a food processor, process for 20 seconds, then pour into a bowl. Refrigerate.

DECORATION AND PRESENTATION: pick over the raspberries. Run the blade of a knife around each custard and unmould on to 4 plates. Pour the sauce around the custards and decorate with the fresh raspberries. Serve immediately.

SAUTÉED BANANAS WITH LIME

SERVES 4

4 small bananas, 200 g/7 oz each
3 limes
juice of 1 orange
1 teaspoon groundnut oil
4 teaspoons Nutrasweet sweetener

Preparation time: 10 minutes
Cooking time: 4 minutes

TO PREPARE THE FRUIT: with a vegetable peeler, peel the zest from 1 lime and cut into very thin julienne. Cook for 4 minutes in a small saucepan of boiling water. Drain in a small sieve and place on a cloth to dry. Peel the bananas, remove the black ends and strings, and cut in half lengthwise.

Squeeze the juice from the limes, combine with orange juice and set aside.

TO COOK THE BANANAS: heat the oil over a medium heat in a large nonstick frying pan. Place the banana halves in the pan, flat side down, and cook for 2 minutes. Turn and cook for 2 minutes more. They should be soft inside, golden brown outside. Add the lime and orange juices and scrape the bottom of the pan with a wooden spoon, being careful not to damage the bananas.

DECORATION AND PRESENTATION: reduce the heat to very low, remove the bananas with a fish slice and place 2 on each of 4 plates. Add the sweetener to the frying pan and mix. Add the lime julienne and heat through. Pour the sauce round the bananas and serve hot or lukewarm.

LIGHT RASPBERRY MILLE-FEUILLES

SERVES 4

BATTER

100 ml/3 ½ fl oz natural yogurt
20 g/¾ oz plain flour
pinch of salt
1 teaspoon groundnut oil

FILLING

¼ vanilla pod
150 ml/¼ pint skimmed milk
20 g/¾ oz cornflour
1 tablespoon cold water
300 g/11 oz raspberries
3 egg whites
10 g/¼ oz granulated sugar
4 teaspoons Nutrasweet sweetener

COULIS

15 g/½ oz raspberries
juice of ½ lemon
2 tablespoons water
2 teaspoons Nutrasweet sweetener

DECORATION

4 sprigs of mint

Preparation time: 30-35 minutes
Cooking time: 8 minutes

TO PREPARE THE FILLING AND THE COULIS: split the vanilla pod lengthwise and place in a saucepan with the skimmed milk. Bring to the boil. Dissolve the cornflour in the water, add to the boiling milk and boil for 1 minute, stirring constantly. Pour the mixture into a bowl, cover with cling film and set aside. Make the coulis (see page 140) and refrigerate.

TO PREPARE AND COOK THE BATTER: place all the ingredients for the batter except the groundnut oil in a food processor and process for 20 seconds. Transfer to a bowl.

Moisten a piece of kitchen paper with the groundnut oil, lightly grease a large nonstick frying pan with it and heat over a low heat. When the pan is hot, pour in ½ teaspoon of the batter on one side of the pan and spread it quickly with the back of a spoon to create a circle 6 cm/2½ inches in diameter.

Quickly make 3 other circles next to each other and cook for 2 minutes. Turn them over and cook the other sides. They should be dry and crisp.

Remove them from the pan and place on a rack. Repeat this step twice so that you have 12 little pancakes.

TO FINISH THE FILLING: pick the raspberries and set aside.

In a bowl, beat the egg whites until very stiff, adding the sugar and sweetener a little at a time. Beat the reserved milk and cornflour mixture, then gently fold in the egg whites.

TO FINISH THE MILLE-FEUILLES: place 4 little pancakes on a work surface. Place some of the filling on each one and top with a layer of raspberries. Place another pancake on top, again cover with the filling and a layer of raspberries and finish with a pancake dusted with sweetener.

PRESENTATION: place a mille-feuille on each serving plate, surround with the raspberry coulis, decorate each with a sprig of mint and serve.

Note: you can prepare the pancakes in advance as long as you place them in a tin so that they stay crisp and dry.

Light Raspberry Mille-Feuilles

POACHED PEARS WITH CHOCOLATE SAUCE

SERVES 4

4 Comice pears
1 litre/1 ¾ pints water
juice of 1 lemon
½ vanilla pod

SAUCE
100 ml/3 ½ fl oz skimmed milk
½ vanilla pod
5 tablespoons unsweetened cocoa powder
6 teaspoons Nutrasweet sweetener

Preparation time: 5-6 minutes
Cooking time: 15 minutes

TO PREPARE AND COOK THE PEARS: peel the pears with a vegetable peeler, keeping the stalks intact. Place upright in a saucepan, add the water, lemon juice and ½ vanilla pod and bring to the boil. Reduce the heat and simmer gently for 15 minutes.

Remove the pears with a slotted spoon and place on a board.

TO PREPARE THE SAUCE: pour the milk into a small saucepan. Split the ½ vanilla pod and scrape the seeds into the milk. Add the cocoa powder and bring to the boil, beating constantly; continue beating and boil for 1 minute. Dissolve the sweetener in the chocolate sauce.

DECORATION AND PRESENTATION: dip the hot pears into the chocolate sauce and turn them to coat well. Place them on a platter, surround with the remaining sauce and serve hot or lukewarm.

RICE PUDDING WITH DRIED APRICOTS AND FRESH APRICOT SAUCE

SERVES 4

75 g/3 oz short-grain rice
50 g/2 oz dried apricots
1 vanilla pod
500 ml/17 fl oz skimmed milk
knob of butter or margarine
6 teaspoons Nutrasweet sweetener

SAUCE
200 g/7 oz fresh apricots
100 ml/3 ½ fl oz water
6 teaspoons Nutrasweet sweetener

DECORATION
150 g/5 oz fresh apricots
4 sprigs of mint

Preparation time: 35 minutes
Cooking time: 35 minutes, 3 hours before serving; sauce:
10 minutes

TO PREPARE THE RICE AND THE DRIED APRICOTS: split the vanilla pod in half lengthwise and place in a saucepan with the rice and milk. Bring to the boil. Reduce the heat and simmer gently for about 30 minutes, stirring from time to time with a wooden spatula. The milk should be absorbed by the rice and the mixture should be creamy. While the rice is cooking, cut the dried apricots into 3 mm/⅛ inch dice and set aside.

TO PREPARE THE MOULDED PUDDINGS: transfer the cooked rice to a dish, remove the vanilla pod and leave to cool for 15 minutes. Use the butter or margarine to grease 4 small ramekin dishes. When the rice is cool, carefully fold in the diced apricots and the sweetener. Divide the mixture between the ramekins and tap each on the work surface to level them out. Place in the refrigerator for at least 3 hours.

TO PREPARE THE SAUCE: quarter the 200 g/7 oz fresh apricots and remove the stones. Cook gently for 10 minutes with the water. When they are tender, add the sweetener and mix. Process for 20 seconds in a food processor and pour the purée into a bowl. Refrigerate.

DECORATION AND PRESENTATION: cut each of the remaining fresh apricots in 8 and remove the stones. Dip the bottoms of the ramekins in very hot water for 5 seconds. Unmould on to the centre of 4 plates. Surround each pudding with the apricot sauce, covering the bottom of the plates. Decorate the puddings by surrounding them with the apricot sections and stud each pudding with a sprig of fresh mint.

MELON WITH JURANÇON WINE

SERVES 4

2 Charentais melons
250 ml/8 fl oz sweet Jurançon wine (from the Pau region of France)
100 g/4 oz redcurrants
1 pink grapefruit, peeled and segmented
4 sprigs of mint

Preparation time: 15 minutes

TO PREPARE THE FRUIT: with a fork, stem the redcurrants. Cut the melons in half and scrape out the seeds with a teaspoon. Cut each half in three. Peel each piece with a small sharp knife. Slice the melon into thin crescents.

DECORATION AND PRESENTATION: arrange the melon slices in 4 shallow bowls like the petals of a flower. Place some grapefruit segments and redcurrants in the middle of each flower and douse with wine. Before serving, place the bowls in the freezer for 5 minutes so that the fruit is ice cold. Decorate the redcurrants with a sprig of mint and serve.

Melon with Jurançon Wine

CHOCOLATE RAVIOLI WITH ORANGE SAUCE

SERVES 4

RAVIOLI DOUGH

20 g/¾ oz unsweetened cocoa powder
100 g/4 oz plain flour
50 g/2 oz egg white

FILLING

65 g/2½ oz stoned prunes
15 g/½ oz toasted flaked almonds
2 tablespoons 0% fat fromage frais
pinch of powdered cinnamon

SAUCE

2 oranges
300 ml/½ pint orange juice
½ vanilla pod
5 teaspoons Nutrasweet sweetener
1 tablespoon cornflour
1 tablespoon cold water

Preparation time: 35-40 minutes
Cooking time: 5 minutes

TO PREPARE THE DOUGH: place all the ingredients for the dough in a food processor and process for 20 seconds. Place the dough on a board and form into 2 balls. With a floured rolling pin, roll out 2 very thin pieces, less than 2 mm/1/12 inch thick. Cover the dough with a tea towel and set aside.

TO PREPARE THE FILLING: place all the ingredients for the filling in a food processor and process for 15 seconds. Transfer to a bowl.

TO PREPARE THE RAVIOLI: with a very sharp knife, cut 12 rectangles of dough measuring about 7.5 cm × 6 cm/3 × 2½ inches. Divide the filling into 12 little balls and place them in the centre of each rectangle of dough. Lightly moisten the edges of the rectangles with water and fold the dough over

Chocolate Ravioli with Orange Sauce

the stuffing, making sure there is no air in the pockets. Press the edges closed. Make a decorative border around each one with a pastry wheel and set aside.

TO PREPARE THE SAUCE: remove the zest of 1 orange with a vegetable peeler, cut into fine julienne and set aside. Peel and segment both oranges (see page 149) and set aside.

Pour the orange juice into a saucepan, add the vanilla pod and sweetener and bring to the boil. Add the cornflour dissolved in the cold water. Allow to thicken while stirring constantly, then lower the heat to a simmer. Simmer for 5 minutes. Remove the vanilla pod.

TO COOK THE RAVIOLI: quickly place the ravioli one by one in a large saucepan of boiling water. As soon as the water begins to boil again, reduce the heat and cook them in barely simmering water for 5 minutes. Carefully remove with a slotted spoon and drain on a tea towel.

DECORATION AND PRESENTATION: 3 minutes before the ravioli have finished cooking, add the julienned orange zest and orange segments to the sauce. Arrange 3 ravioli on each plate and pour the sauce round, with equal quantities of julienned zest and orange segments. Serve hot or warm.

LITTLE CHOCOLATE CUSTARDS

SERVES 4

500 ml/17 fl oz skimmed milk
40 g/1 ½ oz unsweetened cocoa powder
½ vanilla pod, split in 2 lengthwise
5 egg whites
16 teaspoons Nutrasweet sweetener

Preparation time: 5 minutes
Cooking time: 25 minutes, 2 hours in advance

TO PREPARE THE CUSTARDS: place the milk, cocoa powder and vanilla pod in a saucepan. Bring to the boil, beating well to avoid lumps. Reduce the heat and cook for 2 more minutes, stirring constantly. Remove from the heat.

In a bowl, lightly beat the egg whites with a fork without allowing them to foam. Add the sweetener and mix well. Slowly pour in the cocoa and milk mixture while stirring. Skim off any foam that forms on the surface.

FINISHING AND COOKING THE CUSTARDS: preheat the oven to 180°C/350°F/Gas Mark 4. Fill 8 small porcelain custard cups with the mixture. Place in a simmering *bain-marie* and bake in the oven for about 25 minutes. To check if they are cooked, gently shake a custard cup; if the surface trembles slightly, it is ready. Remove from the oven and from the *bain-marie*. Cool for 15 minutes at room temperature, then refrigerate for at least 2 hours before serving.

Note: you can make these custards well in advance since they keep, refrigerated, for up to 3 days.

STRAWBERRY SOUP WITH ORANGE AND WINE SYRUP

SERVES 4

500 g/1 ¼ lb strawberries

SYRUP
4 oranges
500 ml/17 fl oz red wine
juice of 1 lemon
2 tablespoons fresh or frozen blackcurrants
1 clove
1 small cinnamon stick
bunch of mint
14 teaspoons Nutrasweet sweetener

Preparation time: 20-25 minutes
Cooking time: 5 minutes, 6 hours in advance

TO PREPARE THE SYRUP: with a vegetable peeler, remove the zest of 1 orange. Cut into fine julienne, cook for 4 minutes in boiling water, drain on a cloth and set aside.

Peel and segment all the oranges (see page 149) and set aside in a bowl.

Pour the red wine and lemon juice into a small saucepan. Add the blackcurrants, clove, cinnamon and 2-3 stems from the bunch of mint. Bring to the boil and cook over a high heat for 5 minutes.

Pass the wine mixture through a fine-mesh sieve on to the orange segments. Add the sweetener and leave to cool for 30 minutes at room temperature. Refrigerate for at least 6 hours.

PRESENTATION: wash and hull the strawberries.

Cut half the strawberries into thin slices and arrange around the edges of 4 plates. Quarter the remaining strawberries and place in the centre of the plates. Pour a ladleful of marinated orange segments over the strawberries and garnish with the julienned zest.

Finely chop several mint leaves and sprinkle over the plates. Decorate with small mint sprigs and serve.

EXOTIC FRUIT SOUP WITH LAVENDER

SERVES 4

1 small pineapple, about 500 g/1 ¼ lb
1 papaya
1 mango

SYRUP

2 tablespoons fresh or dried lavender flowers
2 passion fruit
1 litre/1 ¾ pints water
2 large sprigs of mint
½ vanilla pod
1 clove
2.5 cm/1 inch piece of cinnamon stick
1 lime
1 lemon
12 teaspoons Nutrasweet sweetener

DECORATION

2 kiwi fruit
4 sprigs of mint
pinch of lavender flowers

Preparation time: 20-25 minutes
Cooking time: syrup: 10 minutes, at least 1 hour in advance

TO PREPARE THE SYRUP: scrape out the pulp and seeds from the passion fruit and place in a saucepan. Add the water, lavender flowers, mint, vanilla, clove and cinnamon. Bring to the boil, then reduce the heat to barely simmering.

With a vegetable peeler, remove a third of the zest of both the lime and lemon, place in the saucepan and add their juice as well. Cook for 8 minutes. Remove from the heat and leave to cool at room temperature for 30 minutes. Add the sweetener, mix with a whisk and strain through a fine-mesh sieve. Set aside in the refrigerator.

TO PREPARE THE FRUIT: peel the pineapple, cut in 6 and remove the core. Peel the papaya, cut in half lengthwise and scrape away the seeds with a teaspoon. Peel the mango and

slice the fruit away from the stone.

Cut each fruit in very thin slices, about 3 mm/⅛ inch thick. Add to the syrup and refrigerate for at least 1 hour.

DECORATION AND PRESENTATION: peel the kiwi fruit and slice thinly. Divide the fruit soup between 4 dessert bowls or shallow soup plates. Decorate with kiwi slices, a sprig of mint and a pinch of lavender flowers.

SOUFFLÉED RASPBERRY SOUP

SERVES 8

150 g/5 oz raspberries
300 g/11 oz pears cooked in syrup (see page 150)
15 g/½ oz Nutrasweet sweetener
½ teaspoon Kirsch
dash of lemon juice
2 egg yolks
7 egg whites
20 g/¾ oz softened butter

RASPBERRY COULIS
200 g/7 oz raspberries
10 g/¼ oz Nutrasweet sweetener
100 ml/3 ½ fl oz water
juice of 1 lemon

Preparation time: 40-45 minutes
Cooking time: 5 minutes

TO PREPARE THE RASPBERRY COULIS: dissolve the 10 g/¼ oz sweetener in the water in a small pan. Boil until a syrup is obtained. Purée the 200 g/7 oz raspberries in a food processor and pass through a fine-mesh sieve, stirring to help it pass through.

Mix the raspberry purée with the syrup and add the lemon juice. Transfer to a bowl and set aside.

TO PREPARE THE SOUFFLÉ MIXTURE: in a food processor blend together the drained pears, sweetener, Kirsch, dash of lemon juice and egg yolks. Pour the purée into a bowl.

With a pastry brush, grease 8 individual soufflé dishes with the softened butter.

Beat the egg whites in a bowl with a whisk until soft peaks form. Fold a quarter of the egg whites into the pear purée, then fold in the remaining egg whites.

COOKING AND PRESENTATION: preheat the oven to 160°C/ 325°F/Gas Mark 3. Divide the whole raspberries among the 8 soufflé dishes. Pour a tablespoon of raspberry coulis on top of the raspberries. Then fill with the soufflé mixture. Run your thumb around the inner edges of the dishes to allow the soufflé to rise easily. Cook for 5 minutes in the oven. Serve immediately and present the remaining raspberry coulis in a sauceboat.

FROTHY CITRUS FRUIT GRATIN

SERVES 4

2 oranges
2 pink grapefruit
2 yellow grapefruit

SABAYON
juice of 2 oranges
2 eggs
6 teaspoons Nutrasweet sweetener

DECORATION
4 sprigs of mint

Preparation time: 20-25 minutes
Cooking time: 4 minutes; sabayon: 4-5 minutes

TO PREPARE THE FRUIT: peel each citrus fruit completely; that is, with a sharp knife, first cut off both ends, exposing the flesh. Stand the fruit on one end and cut off slices from top to bottom, removing all the rind, pith and membrane. Then, cut each segment away from the dividing membrane. Save the juice that is released.

Frothy Citrus Fruit Gratin

Arrange the orange and grapefruit segments in the form of a flower on 4 individual gratin dishes, alternating the colours. Preheat the grill.

TO PREPARE THE SABAYON: pour the juice saved from the citrus fruit into a sauté pan and add the juice of the 2 oranges. Beat the eggs in a bowl and add to the sauté pan, beating well until the eggs are foamy. Place the pan over a medium heat and continue to beat with a whisk, using a figure-of-eight motion, for about 4-5 minutes, or until the eggs have thickened and increased in volume. Remove from the heat, beat in the sweetener and pour some of the mixture over each gratin dish of fruit.

DECORATION AND PRESENTATION: place the gratin dishes under the grill for ½-1 minute. When they have browned slightly, remove. Place the dishes on individual plates, decorate each with a sprig of mint and serve immediately.

Note: you can replace the citrus fruit with any other seasonal fruit.

PEAR AND CINNAMON TARTS

SERVES 4

4 ripe pears, about 120 g/4½ oz each
4 punches of powdered cinnamon
750 ml/1¼ pints water
50 g/2 oz Nutrasweet sweetener
1 vanilla pod
4 rounds fresh or frozen puff pastry, 13 cm/5 inches
diameter and 3 mm/⅛ inch thick (about 20 g/¾ oz each)

DECORATION
4 mint leaves
4 small pieces of cinnamon stick

Preparation time: 25-30 minutes
Cooking time: 20-25 minutes

TO PREPARE AND COOK THE PEARS: peel the pears and cut off the tops with the stalks intact. Reserve the tops. Halve the pears lengthwise and core.

Mix the water and sweetener in a saucepan. Add the vanilla pod and bring to the boil. Place the pear halves in the syrup and cook for about 15 minutes. Drain and reserve both the syrup and pears.

TO PREPARE THE TARTS: preheat the oven to 160°C/325°F/Gas Mark 3.

Place the pastry rounds on a nonstick baking sheet. Prick with a fork. Cut the pear halves lengthwise into thin slices and arrange them in circles on the pastry rounds, leaving a border of 1 cm/½ inch. Place a pear top with its intact stalk in the centre of each circle. Dust each tart with the cinnamon.

COOKING AND PRESENTATION OF THE TARTS: bake the tarts for about 8 minutes. To serve, place each tart on a plate and brush with a little of the reserved syrup to make the fruit shine. Decorate with a mint leaf and a small piece of cinnamon stick.

APPLE TART

SERVES 4

PASTRY
25 g/1 oz plain flour
25 g/1 oz oat flakes
25 ml/1 fl oz water
pinch of salt
½ teaspoon groundnut oil

FILLING
3 Granny Smith apples
small knob of chilled butter
3 teaspoons Nutrasweet sweetener

Preparation time: 15 minutes
Cooking time: about 18 minutes

TO PREPARE THE PASTRY: place the flour and oats in a food processor and process for 20 seconds, add the water and salt and process for 15 seconds more. Remove the dough from the processor, form into a ball, wrap in cling film and refrigerate for 20 minutes.

Grease a nonstick baking sheet with a drop of oil. With a lightly floured rolling pin, roll the pastry out into a very thin round. Place on the baking sheet and brush with the peanut oil.

TO PREPARE THE FILLING: preheat the oven to 190°C/375°F/Gas mark 4. Peel, quarter and core the apples. Slice each quarter into very thin crescents. Arrange the apple slices in concentric circles on the dough.

BAKING AND PRESENTATION: bake the tart for 15 minutes. Remove from the oven and run the chilled butter, stuck on the end of a fork, over the apples. Place the tart under a preheated grill for a moment to lightly brown the apples. Slide the tart on to a platter, sprinkle with the sweetener and serve immediately.

SORBETS AND FROZEN DESSERTS

CAMOMILE AND HONEY SORBET

To make sorbets easier to prepare, it is useful to own a small electric ice-cream/sorbet maker. You can also get good results by placing the sorbet mixture in metal ice-cube trays and freezing. Immediately before serving, blend the sorbet in a food processor for 1 minute only.
Sorbets prepared without sugar should be served as soon as they are frozen. Added sugar acts as an anti-freezing agent; without it, a long period in the freezer can destroy the sorbet's fresh taste.

SERVES 4

4 tablespoons (or 5 teabags) camomile flowers
75 g/3 oz honey
750 ml/1 ¼ pints water
juice of 1 orange
juice of 1 lemon
8 teaspoons Nutrasweet sweetener

Preparation time: 5 minutes
Freezing time: 15-30 minutes in a sorbet maker; 2 hours in a container

TO PREPARE THE CAMOMILE: bring the water to the boil and add the camomile flowers or teabags. Steep for 20 minutes off the heat.

TO PREPARE THE SORBET: strain the camomile tea through a fine-mesh sieve into a food processor. Add the orange and lemon juice, together with the honey and sweetener. Process for 25 seconds. Transfer to a sorbet maker or metal ice-cube tray and freeze.

PRESENTATION: with a tablespoon, divide the sorbet among 4 dessert goblets and serve immediately.

STRAWBERRY SORBET

SERVES 4

750 g/1 ¾ lb strawberries
juice of 1 lemon
8 teaspoons Nutrasweet sweetener

DECORATION
4 mint leaves

Preparation time: 7 minutes
Freezing time: 15-30 minutes in a sorbet maker; 2 hours in a container

TO PREPARE THE SORBET: wash, dry and hull the strawberries. Place them in a food processor with the lemon juice and sweetener. Process for 25 seconds, transfer to a sorbet maker or metal ice-cube tray and freeze.

DECORATION AND PRESENTATION: with a tablespoon, divide the sorbet among 4 dessert goblets. Decorate with a mint leaf and serve immediately.

APPLE AND CINNAMON SORBET

SERVES 4

1 kg/2¼ lb Granny Smith apples
½ teaspoon powdered cinnamon
juice of 3 limes
zest of 1 lime
100 ml/3½ fl oz water
12 teaspoons Nutrasweet sweetener

Preparation time: 20 minutes
Cooking time: 10 minutes
Freezing time: 15-30 minutes in a sorbet maker; 2 hours in a
container

TO PREPARE THE APPLES: peel, quarter and core the apples. Place in a saucepan with the lime juice, zest, water and cinnamon. Cook, covered, over a medium heat for 10 minutes.

TO PREPARE THE SORBET: transfer the apple mixture to a food processor and process for 20 seconds until very smooth. Pour into a bowl, mix in the sweetener and leave to cool for 30 minutes. Place in a sorbet maker or metal ice-cube tray and freeze.

Note: you can present this sorbet in another way: slice the tops off the apples and remove the flesh with a melon baller, being careful not to break the skin. Set the apple shells aside in the freezer. Prepare the sorbet as above, removing the cores and pips from the pulp first. When ready to serve, fill the apple shells with the sorbet and replace the lids.

KIWI FRUIT SORBET

SERVES 4

1 kg/2¼ lb kiwi fruit
juice of 1 orange
juice of 1 lemon
8 teaspoons Nutrasweet sweetener

DECORATION
10 strawberries, cut in half
4 sprigs of mint

Preparation time: 10 minutes
Freezing time: 15-20 minutes in a sorbet maker; 2 hours in a
container

TO PREPARE THE KIWI FRUIT: peel the kiwi fruit. Thinly slice 4 of them and set aside in the refrigerator.

TO PREPARE THE SORBET: quarter the remaining kiwi fruit and place in a food processor. Add the orange and lemon juice and the sweetener. Process for 20 seconds. Pass the mixture through a fine-mesh sieve, pressing down on the fruit with the back of a spoon to extract all the juice. Pour into a sorbet maker or metal ice-cube tray and freeze.

DECORATION AND PRESENTATION: remove the kiwi slices from the refrigerator. Arrange on 4 plates. Place an oval ball of sorbet, formed with a tablespoon, on top of each one. Decorate with the strawberry halves and mint sprigs and serve immediately.

Kiwi Fruit Sorbet

FROZEN MERINGUE NAPOLEON WITH STRAWBERRY SORBET AND FROMAGE FRAIS ICE CREAM

SERVES 4

MERINGUE
5 egg whites
20 g/³⁄₄ oz icing sugar
15 g/¹⁄₂ oz Nutrasweet sweetener

FROMAGE FRAIS ICE-CREAM
250 g/9 oz 0% fat fromage frais
200 ml/7 fl oz water
25 g/1 oz Nutrasweet sweetener
10 g/¹⁄₄ oz cooked lemon zest

STRAWBERRY SORBET
300 g/11 oz ripe, fragrant strawberries, hulled
150 ml/¹⁄₄ pint water
20 g/³⁄₄ oz Nutrasweet sweetener
juice of 1 lemon

MANGO COULIS
1 ripe mango
100 ml/3¹⁄₂ fl oz orange juice
10 g/¹⁄₄ oz Nutrasweet sweetener

DECORATION
4 sprigs of mint
200 g/7 oz strawberries

Preparation time: 35-40 minutes
Cooking time: 2 hours

TO PREPARE AND COOK THE MERINGUE: preheat the oven to 110°C/225°F/Gas Mark ¼. On a sheet of baking parchment the size of a baking sheet, trace 12 7 cm/2¾ inch circles with a pencil.

With a whisk, begin by lightly beating the egg whites in a bowl for 1 minute. Then beat more energetically, lifting the whisk higher to incorporate more air. When the whites begin to stiffen (the whisk should leave traces in the mixture), add the icing sugar and beat rapidly until the whites are stiff and smooth. Finally, sprinkle in the sweetener and fold in gently with a wooden spoon.

Fill a piping bag fitted with a flat nozzle with the meringue and cover the circles drawn on the baking parchment, starting from the centre of each circle and making concentric circles outward. The meringue should be no higher than 5 mm/¹⁄₄ inch. Bake for 2 hours, leaving the oven door slightly ajar.

TO PREPARE THE FROMAGE FRAIS ICE-CREAM: boil together the water and sweetener; leave to cool.

In a bowl, mix together the *fromage frais*, cooked lemon zest and cooled sugar syrup. Transfer to a sorbet maker and freeze.

TO PREPARE THE STRAWBERRY SORBET: boil together the water and sweetener; leave to cool.

Purée the strawberries in a food processor. Thin with the sugar syrup and lemon juice. Transfer to a sorbet maker and freeze.

TO PREPARE THE MANGO COULIS: peel the mango, halve and remove the stone. Cut the mango into pieces. Purée in a food processor with the orange juice and sweetener. Pass through a fine-mesh sieve.

DECORATION AND PREPARATION: pour the mango coulis on to 4 dessert plates, spreading it with a spoon. Arrange the hulled strawberries in a circle around the edge of each plate. Place 4 meringue circles on a board. Carefully place an oval ball of strawberry sorbet, made with a tablespoon, on each one. Cover each with another circle and place an oval ball of *fromage frais* ice-cream on top. Top with a third meringue circle.

Place each meringue Napoleon on a prepared plate. Decorate with fresh mint and serve immediately.

ICED VACHERIN WITH MIXED RED BERRIES

SERVES 4

MERINGUES
4 egg whites
20 g/³⁄₄ oz icing sugar
15 g/½ oz Nutrasweet sweetener

VANILLA SAUCE
25 g/1 oz skimmed milk powder
250 ml/8 fl oz water
1 vanilla pod
1 tablespoon crème fraîche or double cream
3 egg yolks
15 g/½ oz fruit sugar (fructose –
available in health-food stores)

FROMAGE FRAIS ICE-CREAM
250 g/9 oz 0% fat fromage frais
10 g/¼ oz cooked lemon zest
200 ml/7 fl oz water
25 g/1 oz Nutrasweet sweetener

DECORATION
400 g/14 oz mixed red berries (raspberries, strawberries,
redcurrants and blackberries)
4 sprigs of mint

Preparation time: 30-35 minutes
Cooking time: 2 hours

TO PREPARE THE VANILLA SAUCE: dissolve the skimmed milk powder in the water in a saucepan. Add the vanilla pod, split in half, and the *crème fraîche* or double cream. Slowly bring to the boil.

In a bowl, beat the egg yolks with the fruit sugar until the yolks are very pale yellow. Slowly pour the hot milk into the egg yolks, mixing well. Pour back into the saucepan.

Cook over a low heat, stirring constantly, until the sauce thickens and coats the back of the spoon. Do not allow to boil or the sauce would separate.

When the sauce has thickened, remove from the heat and pass through a fine-mesh sieve into a bowl. Leave to cool, beating from time to time, then refrigerate.

TO PREPARE AND COOK THE MERINGUE: preheat the oven to 110°C/225°F/Gas Mark ¼.

On a piece of baking parchment the size of a baking sheet, draw 4 7.5 cm/3 inch circles with a pencil.

Beat the egg whites into a meringue with the icing sugar and sweetener as described on page 154. Fill a piping bag fitted with a plain nozzle with the meringue and make baskets, using the pencilled circles as a guide. First make a flat circle of meringue using concentric circles; then build the sides with circles placed one on top of the other once you've arrived at the edge. Bake for 2 hours with the oven door slightly ajar.

TO PREPARE THE FROMAGE FRAIS ICE-CREAM: prepare the *fromage frais* ice-cream as described on page 154.

DECORATION AND PRESENTATION: while the meringue baskets are baking, pick over and prepare the selection of berries.

On each plate, place a slightly warm meringue basket, fill with the *fromage frais* ice-cream, pour the vanilla sauce round and arrange the berries on the sauce. Decorate with the sprigs of mint.

POACHED PEACHES WITH RED WINE GRANITA

SERVES 6

6 yellow or white peaches
1 litre/3 ½ pints water
juice of 1 lemon
1 cinnamon stick
6 teaspoons Nutrasweet sweetener
4 sprigs of mint

GRANITA
500 ml/17 fl oz good red wine
juice of 2 small oranges
juice of 1 lemon
12 teaspoons Nutrasweet sweetener

Preparation time: 10 minutes
Cooking time: 5-10 minutes
Freezing time: 4-8 hours

TO PREPARE THE GRANITA: pour the wine, orange and lemon juices and sweetener into a glass bowl. Mix very well and transfer to a shallow freezing tray. Freeze for at least 4 hours, preferably 8, stirring and scraping at regular intervals with a fork to crystallize.

TO PREPARE AND COOK THE PEACHES: wash, but do not peel, the peaches. Place in a saucepan with the water, lemon juice and cinnamon stick. Bring to the boil, then lower the heat and simmer for 5-10 minutes, depending on the size and ripeness of the fruit.
    Transfer the peaches and their cooking liquid in a bowl and add the sweetener. Leave to cool for 30 minutes at room temperature, then refrigerate.

DECORATION AND PRESENTATION: Place 6 dessert goblets in the freezer to chill. Drain the peaches and peel carefully. Remove the granita from the freezer and stir well with a fork to crystallize. Divide the granita between the 6 chilled goblets. Add a poached peach to each goblet and decorate with the mint. Serve.

PINK GRAPEFRUIT GRANITA WITH NOILLY PRAT

SERVES 4

600 ml/1 pint fresh pink grapefruit juice (about 6-7 grapefruit)
150 ml/¼ pint Noilly Prat
juice of 1 lemon
8 teaspoons Nutrasweet sweetener

Preparation time: 10 minutes
Freezing time: about 4 hours

TO PREPARE THE GRANITA: pour the grapefruit juice into a bowl and add the Noilly Prat, lemon juice and sweetener. Beat well. Pour into a long, shallow tray and freeze for about 4 hours, stirring and scraping at regular intervals with a fork.

PRESENTATION: place 4 dessert goblets or champagne glasses in the refrigerator to chill. Remove the granita from the freezer, stir and scrape once more to crystallize, and divide among the goblets. Serve immediately.

FROSTED ORANGES WITH MANDARIN LIQUEUR

SERVES 4

6 juicy oranges
50 ml/2 fl oz mandarin liqueur
juice of 1 lemon
10 teaspoons Nutrasweet sweetener
4 small sprigs of mint

Preparation time: 15 minutes
Freezing time: 4-8 hours

TO PREPARE THE ORANGES: cut a 2 cm/¾ inch-thick cap from the top of 4 of the oranges. With a grapefruit knife, remove

Frosted Oranges with Mandarin Liqueur

the flesh over a bowl, being careful not to break the skin. Place the orange shells and caps in the freezer.

Peel the other 2 oranges and add their flesh to the bowl. Pour the lemon juice over the oranges.

TO PREPARE THE GRANITA: place the orange flesh, mandarin liqueur and sweetener in a food processor. Process for 30 seconds until very smooth.

Pour the mixture through a coarse sieve into a long, shallow tray and freeze for 2-4 hours, stirring and scraping with a fork to crystallize.

DECORATION AND PRESENTATION: remove the orange shells and caps from the freezer. Fill with the granita and top each one with a sprig of mint. Arrange on plates with the caps alongside and serve immediately.

INDEX

PHOTOGRAPHIC ACKNOWLEDGEMENTS

All the photographs in this book were provided by Editions Robert Laffont with the exception of the pictures
appearing on the following pages:
Agence Top/Laurent Rousseau 24, 25; Anthony Blake Photo Library 26; Martin Brigdale 36; Explorer/Michel
Plassart 22, 39; Michel Guérard 8, 9, 10; Michel Guérard/Didier Blanchat 16, Emil Perauer 23, François
Roboth 12; Octopus Publishing Group Ltd/Martin Brigdale 11, 15, 17, 18, 20, 20-21, 35; Sygma/J Pavlovsky
37, P Vauthey 31; Copyright 1976 Time Warner Inc. Reprinted by permission 19.